SIXTH EDITION

Instructor's Manual
to accompany

Educational
Research An Introduction
by Gall, Borg, and Gall

Joyce P. Gall
University of Oregon

Meredith D. Gall
University of Oregon

Longman *Publishers USA*

Instructor's Manual to accompany
Educational Research: An Introduction,
Sixth Edition, by Gall, Borg, and Gall

Longman, 10 Bank Street, White Plains, N.Y. 10606

Associated companies:
Longman Group Ltd., London
Longman Cheshire Pty., Melbourne
Longman Paul Pty., Auckland
Copp Clark Longman Ltd., Toronto

ISBN: 0-8013-0980-8 Title Code: 79272 (Student Book)
ISBN: 0-8013-1227-2 Title Code: 79768 (Instructor's Manual)
ISBN: 0-8013-1782-7 Title Code: 77338 (Student Book with disks)

2 3 4 5 6 7 8 9 10-VG-99989796

CONTENTS

I INTRODUCTION

II TEST ITEM FILE

2

INTRODUCTION

Organization of the Instructor's Manual

The purpose of this manual is to provide you with ideas and resources for teaching a course on educational research using the textbook *Educational Research: An Introduction*, 6th edition.

In this section of the manual, we present ideas and resources for the basic elements of the course: the syllabus, content coverage and sequence, teaching activities, homework, statistics tutorial, and tests. The remaining section of the manual is a test item file containing closed-form and open-form test items, application problems, and teaching activities for each of the 17 chapters of the textbook. The test item file is organized as follows:

   a. Closed-form test items. These items are multiple-choice and matching items that test students' knowledge of specific concepts, procedures, and ideas related to educational research. The items are keyed to the objectives listed at the start of each textbook chapter. For example, if an item begins 1. (obj. 1), that means it is the first item for the chapter and it covers information related to Objective No. 1 in the list of objectives at the beginning of the chapter. The answer is provided below each item.

   b. Open-form test items. These are short-answer items that test students' knowledge of specific concepts, procedures, and ideas related to educational research. The items are similar to the question stems of the closed-form test items, but generally are more challenging because students must construct an answer. Also, each item generally covers more of the content presented in the textbook. Like the closed-form items, each open-form item is keyed to one or more of the objectives listed at the beginning of each textbook chapter. An answer is provided below each item; it often includes more points than the item requests, any of which are acceptable. If desired, you also can include a request for an example in students' answers to the open-form items. Some of the open-form items in the Manual already are written to require an example. For example, item 8 for chapter 3 states, "Explain desensitization, and give an example of a type of study in which it would be necessary." The answer to this item defines desensitization and also provides an example of a type of study that would require this procedure. If you modify items to request examples, it is up to you to judge the acceptability of the examples that students give as part of their answers.

3

c. <u>Application problems</u>. These are the most challenging test items, because students must draw on their knowledge of different parts of the chapter in order to answer them. They generally require more higher-cognitive thinking and judgment than the open-form test items. Because each application problem tests for students' mastery of several concepts, procedures and ideas covered in the chapter, they are not keyed to specific chapter objectives. Application problems can have a variety of acceptable answers, and we include a sample answer to each problem to illustrate an acceptable answer.

d. <u>Teaching activities</u>. We present several activities that you can use during class time when providing instruction about the content of a particular chapter. Only the nucleus of the activity is presented. You can draw on your own expertise and imagination to elaborate on the activity as we described it. Alternatively, the activity may serve as a springboard for thinking of other activities that are more appropriate for your course.

Elements of a Course on Educational Research

<u>Syllabus</u>
Exhibit A at the end of this section presents a syllabus that one of the authors (M. Gall) used in teaching a graduate course (a doctoral-level course that included a few master's level students) using *Educational Research: An Introduction.* It is provided as a possible starting point for your own thinking about how to design a course on educational research and a syllabus describing the course.

<u>Content Coverage</u>
Educational Research: An Introduction, 6th edition, contains 17 chapters and 800 pages of text. This may well be too much content for students to master in a quarter-system course, or even a semester-long course. If so, you can select some of the chapters to cover during the course, and suggest to students that they read the other chapters after the course as the information becomes relevant to their research endeavors. In fact, instructors tell us that many students hold on to the textbook after they take the course and use it as a reference work. The addition of a glossary and the expanded coverage of research topics in the sixth edition (especially in the area of qualitative research) should make the book even more useful for this purpose.

Another approach to content coverage is to provide instruction on all or most of the chapters of the textbook but to assign only certain sections of each chapter. For example, the chapter on correlational research presents basic correlational designs in the first part of the chapter and more sophisticated designs (e.g., path analysis) and statistical issues later in the chapter. You might require students to read only the first part of the chapter and then

4

provide an overview in class of the material covered in later parts of the chapter. If you decide on this approach to content coverage, you can refer to the detailed table of contents in the textbook to decide which topics in each chapter to cover.

Content Sequence

There are two different approaches to sequencing the content of *Educational Research: An Introduction*, 6th edition for a course on research methods. One is a bottom-up approach, in which you teach the various parts of the research process and gradually build to the overall process. Following this approach, you might assign chapters 1 through 9 in order. Then you would provide instruction on selected research designs that are presented in Parts IV, V, and VI. For example, students first would have learned about sampling techniques in chapter 6. Then they could see how these sampling techniques are used in various types of research, such as case studies (chapter 14) and experimental studies (chapters 12 and 13).

In contrast, the top-down approach involves starting the course by helping students develop the "big picture" of educational research. Later in the course you can help them fill in the details. Following this approach, you might start off with chapter 1 and then assign chapters that present complete research designs, for example: descriptive and causal-comparative designs (chapter 10), experimental designs (chapters 12 and 13), case study research (chapter 14) and evaluation research (chapter 17). Then you could teach particular aspects of the research process, such as ethical procedures (chapter 3), reviewing the literature (chapter 4), and collecting data with questionnaires and interviews (chapter 8).

We do not know whether the top-down or bottom-up approach is superior. However, we are fairly certain that you need to focus on both the "big picture" and specialized procedures in order for students to develop a strong initial understanding of educational research.

Teaching Activities

Instructors typically spend some class time reviewing homework assignments, answering students' questions, and explaining ideas presented in the textbook. In addition, they conduct class activities that are specific to particular chapters of the assigned textbook. As we stated above, each of the following 17 sections presents ideas for teaching activities that are specific to a particular chapter.

As a general recommendation, we suggest that you require students to read assigned research articles as homework and then discuss the articles in class throughout the course. Many of the educators who are your students will have had little or no experience in reading original research studies (primary sources) prior to your course. If they have had exposure to educational research, it typically is based on reading digests of research findings in textbooks, newspapers, or practitioner journals. By having students read studies reported in research journals, you will help them learn the source of these research digests. Also, you will give students practice in applying the concepts, procedures, and ideas that they are reading about in the textbook.

You also can give students practice in designing research by having them read an article in a research journal and then asking such questions as, "How could this study have been designed better?" and "How would you design a study to respond to the issues and questions posed as needs for further research?" The syllabus presented in Exhibit A makes reference to nine research studies that students are expected to read in conjunction with selected chapters from the textbook.

There are many appropriate research journals from which to select the articles for students to read. Some of the journals that we have found particularly useful for this purpose include the *American Educational Research Journal, Journal of Educational Research, Journal of Experimental Education, International Journal of Qualitative Studies in Education* , and *Anthropology and Education Quarterly.*

Another helpful source of research articles is the book *Complementary Methods for Research in Education,* edited by Richard M. Jaeger and published in 1988 by the American Educational Research Association (1230 17th Street, NW, Washington, DC 20036, phone 202-223-9485). It includes a variety of research studies with brief introductions by authorities in their respective fields of inquiry. The studies represent the following types of research: history, philosophy, ethnography, case study, and experimentation (both experiments with random assignment and quasi-experiments).

Another source of research articles is our book *Applying Educational Research: A Practical Guide,* 3rd edition, published in 1993 by Longman. It includes articles originally published in research journals, commentary by the author of each article, and notes to clarify technical terms in the articles. The studies represent the following types of research: case study, description, causal-comparison, correlation, experimentation, evaluation, and action research.

Homework

The closed-form items, open-form items, and application problems within the test item file in this manual can be given as homework assignments. The application problems are particularly appropriate for this purpose. Also, there are multiple closed-form and open-form items for most of the objectives of each textbook chapter. Therefore, you might consider assigning some of the items for particular objectives as homework and using the other items for those objectives in tests.

When assigning textbook chapters for students to read as homework, you might advise them to read the objectives at the start of each textbook chapter before studying the chapter. After reading the chapter, students can check their mastery of the chapter by returning to the objectives and checking whether they can remember the concepts, procedures, and ideas associated with each objective. Students also can check their mastery of the textbook content by completing the self-check test at the end of each chapter.

You also can advise students to take special note of the terms that are bold-faced in each chapter. Many of these terms are the subject of the closed-form and open-form items in this manual. Each boldfaced term is defined in the text of the chapter and also in the glossary at the end of the textbook.

As we indicated above, it is important for students to learn how to read articles in research journals. Therefore, you might ask students to read such articles as homework assignments and to prepare written answers to questions that you have prepared about the article. For example, you might ask students to identify the study's research design, variables, data collection procedure for each variable, sampling technique, data analysis procedure, main findings, implications of the findings, and strengths and weaknesses of the study.

Some instructors wish to encourage a personal response to research methodology. If this is one of your goals, you may wish to give students the assignment of maintaining a personal journal of reflections on their textbook readings.

You may be teaching students who are in the process of planning their own research study for a thesis or dissertation. If so, you might want to design homework assignments that give students practice in developing various parts of a research proposal. Exhibit B at the end of this section of the manual provides a form that stimulates students to think about various parts of a research proposal. Because the form is in outline form, students can focus on the substance of the research design rather than on writing style.

One of us (M. Gall) has regularly used the form in Exhibit B when teaching a course on research methods. He assigns different parts of the form depending on which chapter is being studied. As each new part of the form is completed, the student turns in that part of the form plus previously completed parts, so that the instructor can study the emerging proposal and give the students feedback on it.

Some students will want to change their research topic as the course proceeds. We recommend that you give students this option, but ask them to redo as necessary all parts of the proposal plan that you previously assigned. Because the plan is in outline form (see Exhibit B), this task can be completed fairly quickly.

Some students in Dr. Gall's courses who have completed this research proposal form have been able to use it as the basis of their actual dissertation proposal.

Statistics Tutorial

In many settings, instructors find that students come to the research methods course with uneven backgrounds in basic statistical concepts. Some have just taken a statistics course and mastered the concepts, others took statistics long ago and have forgotten many of the concepts, and others may never have taken an appropriate course. Rather than using class time to review (or teach for the first time) statistical concepts, you might suggest that students use the *Longman Statistics Tutorial: A Review of Basic Concepts* by Thomas Rocklin, University of Iowa. This is a computer tutorial that runs under either the Macintosh operating system or Windows and covers key concepts in univariate descriptive statistics, the interpretation of correlations, and main effects and interactions in factorial designs. The tutorial can be ordered by calling Longman Publishers at 1-800-552-2499.

Perhaps the most effective use of the tutorials is to administer a brief pretest and use the results to suggest particular portions of the tutorial to individual students. Some students who are uncomfortable with statistics probably will want to complete the tutorial, no matter how they score on the pretest or what their prior statistics training has been. Completing each tutorial will take less than an hour for most students (longer for those with less solid backgrounds), so it may be a good idea simply to assign them to all students early in the semester. The tutorials are designed to be simple for students to run, either in a computer laboratory or on their own home computer.

Test Item File

The next section of this manual is a test item file for each chapter of the textbook. As stated above, the closed-form and open-form items are keyed to the objectives listed at the start of each chapter in the textbook. Therefore, it is relatively easy to develop tests for the chapters or parts of chapters that you expect students to master.

One method of testing that we have found works well with graduate students is to assign take-home tests consisting of application problems, such as those we include in the next section. These problems are sufficiently complex and open-ended that various responses are possible. You can allow students to study the problems together, but require them to write individual responses to each problem. This procedure encourages students to think about the textbook content in depth, without the anxiety generated by the prospect of a sit-down test. Also, this procedure gives students the opportunity to work both collaboratively (they can study the problems together) and independently (they must write their own responses to each problem on the test).

Note to the Instructor

We welcome feedback on any of the ideas presented in this manual or in the textbook *Educational Research: An Introduction*, 6th edition. You can write to either Meredith (Mark) or Joyce (Joy) Gall at: University of Oregon, College of Education, Eugene, OR 97403. Alternatively, you can write to us at our e-mail address (mgall@oregon.uoregon.edu).

EXHIBIT A

EXAMPLE OF A SYLLABUS FOR A COURSE ON
EDUCATIONAL RESEARCH

CI 612 INTRODUCTION TO RESEARCH DESIGN
CRN 7172   224 Condon School
Tues and Thurs   3:30-4:50 PM

Fall 19--

Instructor: _____
Office: _____ (phone: _____)
My office hours are _____.

Overview

This course has three goals: (1) to increase your understanding of research concepts and procedures, (2) to develop your appreciation of the importance of research in education, and (3) to develop your skill in preparing a research proposal for the doctoral dissertation. I will emphasize how research concepts and procedures apply to dissertation-level studies in education.

Research typically involves several stages: planning (e.g., the dissertation proposal), pilot study and development of measurement tools, data collection and analysis, and report-writing (i.e., writing the dissertation). This course cannot develop your skill in completing all these stages of a research study. These skills are best developed through actual practice in doing research, preferably guided by an experienced researcher. Therefore, the course will focus on the preparation of a dissertation proposal. This is one of the most critical phases of research, because it provides the *blueprint* for all the later stages of the study. The later stages will be covered in this course insofar as they relate to the research proposal.

Course Objectives

This course is intended to help you develop:

1. Understanding of the nature, purposes, and types of educational research.
2. Understanding of procedures for reviewing research literature.
3. Understanding of sampling procedures.
4. Understanding of procedures for selecting and administering tests and other measurement devices
5. Understanding of concepts and procedures relating to: descriptive research, causal-comparative research, correlational research, experimental research, and R & D studies.
6. Understanding of statistical techniques appropriate for analyzing data from different research designs
7. Skill in preparing the various parts of a dissertation proposal.

Course Assignments

The course text is: M. D. Gall, W. R. Borg, & J. P. Gall, *Educational Research: An Introduction*, 6th Edition (New York: Longman, 1996). The following chapters are required reading: Chapters 1, 2, 3, 4, 6, 7, 8, 10, 11, 12, 14, and 15.

Your mastery of these chapters will be tested by sets of take-home application problems. I recommend that you read the other chapters, too, to become familiar with their content for later reference. In addition, you are expected to read a set of 9 research reports that will provide the basis for class discussion. These reports can be purchased as a reading packet from _____ .

A set of take-home application problems will be given to you approximately every two weeks. You can discuss the problems in study groups if you wish, but you need to write your own responses. The application problems are directly related to the objectives at the beginning of each assigned chapter in the text. Follow the typing rules at the end of the syllabus in writing your answers.

Another course requirement is to prepare a research proposal. The proposal does not have to be your actual dissertation problem, although dissertation problems certainly are welcome. Your proposal can be the completion of the outline included in your reading packet or a regular narrative proposal covering the same points as in the reading packet outline. In either case, <u>the assignment must be typed using the typing rules.</u> (If you use the outline, type your responses on the outline; or include the headings of the outline when typing your responses on separate sheets of paper.) This assignment is due on the last scheduled meeting of the course (<u>date</u>). To help you complete the proposal, you will be asked to complete a set of brief exercises based directly on the proposal outline in the reading packet. Each exercise is due one class meeting after the topic to which it pertains has been covered in class.

Class time will be spent in lecture and discussion of actual research studies, dissertation proposal writing, and difficult concepts presented in the textbook.

Grading

Mastery-level performance on the application problems, and a satisfactory research proposal are required to receive an "A." If you do poorly on any assignment, you will be given the option of doing it again.

Class Presentations

The following is a list of topics that will be covered and the textbook chapters to which they are keyed. The dates on which the topics will be discussed are approximate.

		Read beforehand
1. Sept. 24	Introduction to course	
2. Sept. 26	Nature and purpose of educational research	Chapter 1
3. Oct. 1	Comparison of quantitative and qualitative research	Studies 1 & 2
4. Oct. 3	Formulation of a research problem, variables, hypotheses, questions	Chapter 2

TYPING RULES

1. Type all papers.

2. Use a good ribbon on your typewriter or computer printer.

3. If using a computer, print on high-quality mode.

4. Type double-space or space-and-a-half with at least an inch margin on the right or left side.

5. Type using a twelve-point typeface (like this handout). To put it another way, please use a typeface big enough to read easily.

6. Type your name, date, and course title on a cover page or on the upper-right corner of the first page.

7. Paginate the paper. In other words, put a page number on each page of the paper.

8. Use a staple or clamp on the upper left corner to hold the paper together. Do not use clear plastic folders with plastic strip spines to hold your paper together.

9. If you want your paper returned in a confidential manner, submit it in an envelope.

10. If you want your paper mailed to you, submit it in a stamped, self-addressed envelope.

FORM FOR OUTLINING A RESEARCH PROPOSAL

Note: You can give this form to students at the beginning of the course, and ask them to complete various parts of it as you cover concepts, procedures, and ideas that are relevant to those parts.

1. PURPOSE OF STUDY

   A. (One sentence only.) The purpose of this study is to _____ .

   B. What study or literature review is your study most directly based on? (Give citation.)

   C. How does your study build on previous research? (No more than 3 sentences.)

   D. How will your study contribute to knowledge about education?

2. RESEARCH QUESTIONS, HYPOTHESES, AND OBJECTIVES

   A. In what form are you stating your research purposes? (Check one or more.)
   _____ Questions
   _____ Hypotheses
   _____ Objectives

   B. List your research questions/hypotheses/objectives.

   C. Does your study relate to a particular theoretical framework? If it does, describe the framework, and indicate how your research questions, hypotheses, or objectives relate to it.

3. LITERATURE SEARCH

   A. List the descriptors that you will use initially in your literature search.

   B. List the preliminary sources that you will use in your literature search.

4. RESEARCH DESIGN

    A. Describe the research design that you selected for your study: descriptive, causal-comparative, correlational, experimental, case study, or a particular qualitative research tradition.

    B. What are the threats to the internal validity of your research design? What will you do to minimize or avoid these threats?

    C. What are the limitations to the generalizability (i.e., external validity) of the findings that will result from your research design? What will you do to maximize the generalizability of your findings?

5. SAMPLING

    A. Describe the characteristics of the population that you will study, and whether you will sample from this population or study it in its entirety.

    B. Identify your sampling procedure (e.g., simple random sampling), and explain why you selected it.

    C. Indicate the sampling unit (e.g., individual students or a class of students).

    D. Indicate the size of your sample, and explain why that sample size is sufficient.

    E. Indicate whether the sample will be formed into subgroups, and if so, describe the characteristics of the subgroups.

6. VARIABLES

    A. List the variables that you will study. For each variable, indicate whether it is an independent variable, a dependent variable, or neither. If the study is qualitative in nature, indicate the phenomenon you wish to study, the focus of your study, the unit of analysis, if any, and the case or cases that will be the subject of your research report.

7. MEASURES

   A. List the measures that you will select or develop for your study.

   B. For each measure, indicate the variables that it will assess (if it is a quantitative study) or the themes and patterns that it will explore (if it is a qualitative study).

   C. For each measure, indicate which types of validity and reliability are relevant and how you will check them.

8. DATA ANALYSIS PROCEDURES

   A. What statistics, if any, will you use to analyze your data? If your study is qualitative, indicate whether you will use an interpretational, structural, or reflective method of analysis.

9. ETHICS AND HUMAN RELATIONS

   A. What threats, if any, does your study pose for your research participants? What steps will you take to minimize these threats?

   B. How will you gain entry into the setting in which you will collect data?

   C. How will you gain the cooperation of your research participants?

10. TIMELINE
   A. Create a timeline listing in order all the major steps of your study. Also indicate the approximate amount of time that each step will take.

CHAPTER 1
THE NATURE OF EDUCATIONAL RESEARCH

Note: The phrase in parentheses following the item number for both closed-form and open-form items, for example, 1. (obj. 3), refers to the textbook chapter objective to which the item is keyed.

CLOSED-FORM ITEMS

1. (obj. 1) Studies that seek to identify the students who will drop out of high school or the students who will do well in college are examples of
   a. descriptive research.
   b. intervention-oriented research.
   c. prediction research.
   d. theory-building research.
Answer: c

2. (obj. 1) Which of the following statements best reflects the current status of improvement-oriented research?
   a. Researchers have discovered only a few interventions that improve learning.
   b. Researchers have discovered many different types of interventions that improve learning.
   c. Researchers have conducted few improvement-oriented studies in education.
   d. Researchers have not yet conducted studies on forms of cultural oppression that affect student learning.
Answer: b

3. (obj. 2) "Intelligence is that which is measured by intelligence tests." This statement is an example of
   a. an operationally defined construct.
   b. a constitutively defined construct.
   c. a theoretical law.
   d. a grounded theory.
Answer: a

4. (obj. 2) A research hypothesis
   a. can be proved or disproved by a single study.
   b. only can be tested if the constructs have been constitutively defined.
   c. is formulated after the data have been collected.
   d. is formulated before the data have been collected.
Answer: d

5. (obj. 3) The findings of a well-done educational research study
   a. will be value-free.
   b. nonetheless will be value-laden.
   c. nonetheless will have no generalizability beyond the situation that was studied.
   d. will yield clear prescriptions about what ought to be done to improve educational practice.
Answer: b

6. (obj. 4) Which of the following is *not* an example of basic research in education?
   a. Research to identify the parts of the brain that control memory.
   b. Research on physiological changes in students during test-taking situations.
   c. Research on the effects of a pharmaceutical drug on the classroom attention span of students diagnosed with attention-deficit disorder.
   d. Research on factors that explain artistic aptitude.
Answer: c

7. (obj. 5) The view that social reality is independent of those who observe it is a major tenet of
   a. positivism.
   b. postpositivism.
   c. postmodernism.
   d. interpretive research.
Answer: a

8. (obj. 5) Which of the following does *not* typify positivist research?
   a. the study of populations.
   b. the collection of numerical data.
   c. the assumption of an objective social reality.
   d. the assumption that individuals' interpretations of social reality are causal agents.
Answer: d

9. (obj. 6) In writing a research report, the author includes her own reactions to the classrooms she has studied. This style of reporting typifies
   a. positivist research.
   b. scientific realism.
   c. reflexivity in research.
   d. postmodernism.
Answer: c

10. (obj. 7) If a postpositivist researcher was interested in the effects of cooperative learning, he most likely would select for study
   a. a large sample of teachers who were using this method.
   b. a few teachers who were using this method.
   c. every teacher in a school district who was using this method.
   d. a large sample of staff developers who were training teachers in this method.
Answer: b

11. (obj. 8) Postpositivist researchers typically deal with the shortcomings of numerical data by
   a. not subjecting such data to statistical analysis.
   b. collecting such data only on large samples.
   c. making pictorial representations of numerical data.
   d. relying instead on thorough verbal descriptions of phenomena.
Answer: d

12. (obj. 9) The view that the real world consists of layers of causal structures is a primary tenet of
   a. positivism.
   b. postpositivism.
   c. scientific realism.
   d. both postpositivism and scientific realism.
Answer: c

13. (obj. 10) *Qualitative research* sometimes is called
   a. interpretive research.
   b. case study research.
   c. postpositivist research.
   d. all of the above.
Answer: d

14. (obj. 11) The view that qualitative research plays a discovery role in inquiry, whereas quantitative research plays a confirmatory role, assumes that
   a. qualitative research is less valid than quantitative research.
   b. the emic perspective takes precedence over the etic perspective.
   c. quantitative and qualitative research are complementary.
   d. quantitative and qualitative research are incompatible with each other.
Answer: c

15. (obj. 12) A postmodernist would argue that
   a. positivist research is not superior to literary studies.
   b. positivist research is superior to literary studies.
   c. literary studies has a privileged position in the search for truth.
   d. it is necessary to combine literary studies with positivist research in order to make scientific progress.
Answer: a

16. (obj. 13) Refutation tests of knowledge claims would enable a researcher to
   a. prove that theory X is correct and theory Y is wrong.
   b. prove that theory X is wrong and that there is empirical support for theory Y.
   c. make value-free comparisons of theory X and theory Y.
   d. make empirical observations without the need for a prior knowledge claim.
Answer: b

17. (obj. 13) The notion of progressive discourse in scientific inquiry implies that
   a. social scientists view their work as a moral enterprise.
   b. the tenets of postmodernism are valid.
   c. the tenets of postpositivism are valid.
   d. the social sciences will advance only when social science researchers enter into a constructive dialogue with humanists and artists.
Answer: a

OPEN-FORM ITEMS

1. (obj. 1) 1. Briefly describe four types of knowledge yielded by educational research.
Answer:
    a. *Description.* This is the initial step in new fields of investigation. It depends heavily on the state of measurement in the science.
    b. *Prediction.* Description often reveals relationships between variables. These observed relationships can be used to make predictions with varying degrees of accuracy.
    c. *Improvement or control.* Once predictions of events are possible, researchers can attempt to influence their occurrence by designing appropriate interventions. In education, interventions often have the goal of improving a learning outcome.
    d. *Explanation.* This the ultimate goal of research. The explanations often take the form of theories.

2. (obj. 2) State two reasons why theories are useful.
Answer (any 2 OK):
    a. They identify commonalities among phenomena that otherwise appear unrelated.
    b. They can be used to make accurate predictions of future events.
    c. They can be used to design or implement interventions that have known consequences.

3. (obj. 3) How is D. C. Phillips's distinction between *is* and *ought* relevant to the application of educational research to practice?
Answer:
Research tells practitioners what is but cannot tell them what they ought to do. Knowledge about what is helps practitioners by contributing to their dialogue about what ought to be.

4. (obj. 4) A common criticism of basic research in education is that it seldom leads directly to improvement in educational practice. What are two reasons that basic research nonetheless should be supported?
Answer (any 2 OK):
    a. Even though its immediate impact may be slight, its eventual impact may be great.
    b. Without basic research, we have little chance of gaining a better understanding of the underlying processes involved in education.
    c. Studies in other sciences such as medicine show that basic research contributes more to important advances in practice than all other kinds of investigation.

5. (obj. 5) State one way in which positivists and postpositivists differ in how they view social reality.

Answer (any 1 OK):

a. Positivists believe that social reality is independent of the individuals who observe it, whereas postpositivists believe that social reality is constructed by individuals and therefore does not exist independently of the individuals who observe it.

b. Positivists believe that it is possible to make bias-free observations of social reality, whereas postpositivists believe that bias is inevitable because individuals construct their own interpretations of social reality.

6. (obj. 6) Why do postpositivist researchers distinguish their perspective from the perspectives of the individuals whom they studied and of the individuals who will read their research report?

Answer:

Postpositivist researchers believe that individuals construct their own interpretations of social reality. Therefore, researchers must bear in mind that (a) their interpretations of a social phenomenon may be different from those who participated in the phenomenon and that (b) the way they write their research reports will affect how readers interpret the findings.

7. (obj. 7) Give one reason why postpositivist researchers study cases rather than samples or populations.

Answer (any 1 OK):

a. Postpositivist researchers believe that social reality is constructed locally. Therefore, one must do indepth study of local instances of a phenomenon. Each such instance is a case.

b. Postpositivist researchers believe that social reality is highly variable and changeable, and therefore one must study particular instances of it. Each such instance is a case.

8. (obj. 8) State one criticism of relying on numerical data to measure variables in educational research.

Answer (any 1 OK):

a. Numerical data tend to involve variables that may be of trivial significance in education.

b. The assumption that a numerical value (e.g., the number of students in a classroom as a measure of class size) has the same meaning for all individuals may not be tenable.

9. (obj. 9)
Explain one way in which postpositivists and scientific realists differ in their explanation of the causes of social phenomena.
Answer (any 1 OK):

  a. Postpositivists believe that individuals' interpretations of the social environment are the causes of social phenomena, whereas scientific realists believe that layers of causal structures are the causes of social phenomena.

  b. Postpositivists believe that interpretations are constructed by individuals, whereas scientific realists believe that causal structures are real objects that exist independently of individuals.

10. (obj. 10) State two key differences between quantitative and qualitative research.
Answer (any 2 OK):

  a. In quantitative research, the social environment is an independent reality; in qualitative research, the social environment is constructed by individuals.

  b. In quantitative research, samples are studied; in qualitative research, cases are studied.

  c. In quantitative research, numerical data are emphasized; in qualitative research, verbal data are emphasized.

  d. In quantitative research, instruments are used to measure variables; in qualitative research, the researcher is the "measuring instrument."
(Note: Other answers based on table 1.3 in the textbook also are acceptable)

11. (obj. 11) State one assumption that must be satisfied in order to use quantitative research to verify the findings of a qualitative research study.
Answer (any 1 OK):

  a. The social phenomena being studied must be stable across time and place.

  b. It must be possible to represent the concepts discovered in the qualitative study by a measure that yields numerical scores.

12. (obj. 12) State two key tenets of postmodernism.
Answer (any 2 OK):

  a. It questions the rationality of human action.

  b. It questions the use of positivist epistemology.

  c. It denies that science or any other human endeavor has a privileged position in the search for truth.

  d. It questions whether progress in scientific knowledge is possible.

13. (obj. 13) State two features of social science inquiry that characterize its approach to the search for truth.

Answer (any 2 OK):

    a. Its concepts and procedures are shared and publicly accessible.

    b. Its findings must be replicable in order to be accepted as valid.

    c. Its knowledge claims are subjected to refutability tests.

    d. It has procedures for controlling for error and bias.

    e. It has procedures for determining the generalizability of research findings.

    f. It makes a moral commitment to progressive discourse.

APPLICATION PROBLEMS

Problem 1

Suppose the federal government decides to fund a new program for training high school students in study skills. Some educators argue that all of the appropriated funds should be used to develop model programs and materials, to train teachers in summer institutes, and to hire additional school staff. Other educators argue that at least 15 percent of the appropriations should be allocated for research on study skills. What defense could you offer for the latter proposal?

Sample Answer:

    a. The model programs and materials may be ineffective, in which case the appropriated funds would be wasted. Research is needed to sort out the effective programs from those that are ineffective.

    b. Research may yield new insights about studying and study skills instruction that can be used to develop more effective programs and materials than any that are currently available. This increase in effectiveness is better in the long run than reaching more individuals with less effective programs and materials in the short run.

Problem 2

Suppose you are asked to design a study of teachers' attitudes toward recent school reforms. How would you select a sample and measure teacher attitudes if you were doing (a) a quantitative research study, or (b) a qualitative research study?

Sample Answer:

    a. In the quantitative study, a large sample of teachers that is representative of a defined population would be selected, and their attitudes would be measured by a scale that yields numerical scores.

    b. In the qualitative study, the researchers would select a small number of teachers (or perhaps just one teacher), each of whom would be a case, and their attitudes would be assessed by interviewing the teachers and recording their responses in detail.

TEACHING ACTIVITIES

Activity 1
Identify a report of a quantitative research study and a report of a qualitative research study that are fairly simple. Have students read each study as a homework assignment. In class, have students discuss how the design and the findings of the two studies differ. For purposes of this activity, it does not matter if students understand all the technical details of the study. This activity will help students to discover for themselves how quantitative and qualitative research differ, and to integrate these discoveries with the information about these two approaches presented in chapter 1.

Activity 2
On page 13 of the textbook the authors state that, "putting a research finding into practice also means putting a particular set of values into practice." Assign a research article for all students to read as a homework assignment. In class, have students discuss how the authors' statement applies to this particular study. Having students read a report of an experimental study would be desirable for this particular activity.

CHAPTER 2
DEVELOPING A RESEARCH PROPOSAL

Note: The phrase in parentheses following the item number for both closed-form and open-form items, for example, 1. (obj. 3), refers to the textbook chapter objective to which the item is keyed.

CLOSED-FORM ITEMS

1. (obj. 1) A desire to contribute to research knowledge is a more sound basis for educational research than basing it only on one's personal interests and goals because research knowledge
   a. is represented in the published literature.
   b. is cumulative across studies.
   c. depends on a thorough literature review.
   d. all of the above.
Answer: d

2. (obj. 2) An advantage of theory-based research is that it
   a. allows the researcher to examine any question of personal interest.
   b. provides a rational basis for explaining the research results.
   c. enables the researcher to prove a particular hypothesis.
   d. eliminates the possibility of conflicting interpretations of research findings.
Answer: b

3. (obj. 2) Theory in qualitative research typically involves
   a. formulating a research problem based on an earlier researcher's findings.
   b. discovering a set of constructs, themes, or patterns in the data.
   c. testing hypotheses in accordance with an existing theory.
   d. attempts to disconfirm previously held beliefs about educational phenomena.
Answer: b

4. (obj. 3) The need for replication is more critical in education and other social science disciplines than it is in the physical sciences because
   a. the findings of educational research typically have more practical significance than statistical significance.
   b. dissertation committees expect students in education to carry out research studies that are original in some respect.
   c. the measuring instruments used in the social sciences typically have considerable measurement error.
   d. the social sciences are more concerned with the physical sciences with developing effective interventions.

Answer: c

5. (obj. 4) An advantage of working on a team project in learning to carry out educational research is that
   a. all team members are likely to have similar experience and research interests.
   b. the research problem is likely to be closely allied with the student's interests.
   c. a team project provides insight into how research teams operate.
   d. a team research design typically is simpler than that of a single researcher.

Answer: c

6. (obj. 5) Selecting the research problem for a dissertation study
   a. can take many months of reading, thinking, and talking to others.
   b. usually takes one to two weeks.
   c. is based primarily on one's personal interests.
   d. requires familiarity with theories about the topics that interest you.

Answer: a

7. (obj. 5) Match each section of a research proposal with the appropriate example of the information that is presented in that section.

___ 1. Introduction.
___ 2. Review of literature.
___ 3. Research design.
___ 4. Research method.
___ 5. Data analysis.
___ 6. Human subjects protection.
___ 7. Timeline.

    a. Whether the study will attempt to describe, predict, explain, or control the phenomena being studied.
    b. The methods of data collection to be used.
    c. Statement of the research hypotheses
    d. When each step of the study will be completed.
    e. Critique of the methods used in previous research on the problem
    f. The statistical tests that will be carried out.
    g. Description of how risks to participants will be minimized.

Answer: 1=c, 2=e, 3=a, 4=b, 5=f, 6=g, 7=d

8. (obj. 6) "There is no relationship between parental use of corporal punishment and the level of school misbehavior of third grade students." This is an example of

    a. a null hypothesis.
    b. a research objective.
    c. a research question.
    d. a directional hypothesis.

Answer: a

9. (obj. 6) A directional hypothesis about the relationship between the type of reading instruction and reading comprehension might be stated in terms of

    a. a question as to whether students receiving whole-language instruction or students receiving phonics instruction will score higher on a measure of reading comprehension.
    b. a prediction that there will be no difference in the reading comprehension of students taught by phonics instruction and those taught by whole-language instruction.
    c. a prediction that there will be a difference in the reading comprehension of students taught by phonics instruction and those taught by whole-language instruction, but without specifying which form of instruction will be superior.
    d. a prediction that students taught phonics will have higher reading comprehension scores than students taught by the whole-language method.

Answer: d

10. (obj. 7) The Program Evaluation Review Technique (PERT) is used to
   a. analyze trends in pilot-test data.
   b. select appropriate statistical techniques to analyze research data.
   c. identify and estimate completion times for the major goals and subgoals of a project.
   d. evaluate the results of a research project.
Answer: c

11. (obj. 8) A pilot study of a proposed research study is desirable because
   a. it permits a thorough check of the planned data collection and analysis procedures.
   b. in a pilot study the researcher typically has greater control over the research procedures than in the actual research project.
   c. it permits the researcher to collect enough data before the actual research project that the researcher can predict the likely outcomes.
   d. if the results are positive, further data collection in the research project will be unnecessary.
Answer: a

12. (obj. 9) A dissertation is organized similarly to a research proposal except for the
   a. problem statement.
   b. literature review.
   c. research method.
   d. research findings.
Answer: d

13. (obj. 10) A researcher should base the selection of a journal to which to submit a report of one's research primarily on whether
   a. the journal is willing to publish the report in its original form.
   b. the journal has published other studies dealing with your research topic.
   c. the journal is published by a professional association.
   d. the report covers a topic not previously addressed by this journal.
Answer: b

14. (obj. 11) If your proposal is accepted for presentation at a professional meeting you have an obligation to
   a. also submit the paper to a journal published by the association that is sponsoring the meeting.
   b. attend the meeting and present the paper.
   c. submit the paper to the appropriate ERIC clearinghouse.
   d. prepare a chart essay summarizing your findings.
Answer: b

OPEN-FORM ITEMS

1. (obj. 1) List the five stages of a research study.
Answer:
   a. Identifying a significant research problem.
   b. Writing a research proposal.
   c. Conducting a pilot study.
   d. Conducting the main study.
   e. Preparing a report.

2. (obj. 2) Explain two of the following terms: *theory, construct, operational definition,* and *variable*.
Answer (any 2 OK):
   a. A theory is an explanation of observed events in terms of the structures and processes that are presumed to underlie them.
   b. A construct is a type of concept used by theoreticians to describe a structure or process that is hypothesized to underlie particular observable phenomena.
   c. An operational definition is the definition of a construct in terms of the procedures or operations needed to measure it.
   d. A variable is a construct that can vary in quality or quantity.

3. (obj. 3) List three purposes for doing a replication and extension of a previous study as one's research project.
Answer (any 3 OK):
   a. To check the findings of a "breakthrough" study, i.e. one that challenges previous theory or research.
   b. To check the validity of research findings for a different research population than the one previously studied.
   c. To check trends or changes over time in research findings on a phenomenon.
   d. To check important findings by changing the methods or correcting methodological flaws that were present in the previous study.
   e. To develop and test instructional interventions to the point where they are effective or efficient for practical application.

4. (obj. 4) Give two reasons why working on a team project can be beneficial.
Answer (any 2 OK):

    a. There may be financial support to cover some needed materials or activities.

    b. It may be possible to receive a scholarship or research assistantship that covers most of one's expenses while completing graduate study.

    c. It provides the opportunity for you to participate in a larger, more sophisticated study than one you could do alone.

    d. You have a chance to learn about the dynamics of team research.

    e. You can learn from a variety of other research team members, each of whom brings unique training and experience to the project.

5. (obj. 5) Give two reasons why it is important to write a complete research proposal before undertaking a study.
Answer (any 2 OK):

    a. Composing a proposal compels you to think through and record your planned research design and procedures.

    b. You can more easily find and correct flaws in a written proposal than you can after you have begun collecting data.

    c. University and college faculty usually want to see a complete proposal before authorizing you to begin your study.

6. (obj. 5) List two points that typically are covered in the introductory section of a research proposal.
Answer (any 2 OK):

    a. A complete statement of the research problem to be addressed.

    b. A description of how the proposed study is grounded in the research literature.

    c. Speculation about how the proposed study will contribute to research knowledge and educational practice.

    d. A list of the research hypotheses, questions, or objectives that the study will address.

7. (obj. 6) Why do researchers often state a hypothesis in null form, i.e., that no relationship or difference will be found, even when they expect the opposite?
Answer:
The null hypothesis is used in performing tests of statistical significance.

8. (obj. 7) PERT charts often are used in educational research. What is a PERT chart?
Answer:
A planning chart that shows all of the activities and subgoals that go into achieving a given research goal, along with a time estimate for completion of each activity.

9. (obj. 7) Name two advantages of the use of the Program Evaluation and Review Technique (PERT) in developing a timeline for a research proposal.
Answer (any 2 OK):

    a.   PERT allows the researcher to see clearly the relationships among the various activities that the study involves.

    b.   PERT enables the researcher to check her progress and identify activities that must be changed or speeded up in order to keep the project on schedule.

    c.   PERT helps the researcher focus on potential or actual problems that are involved in carrying out the study.

10. (obj. 8) Describe the nature and purpose of a pilot study in educational research.
Answer:
A pilot study involves small-scale testing of the procedures that you plan to use in the main study. The purpose of the pilot study is to identify weaknesses in the planned procedures so that the researcher can design better procedures for use in the main study.

11. (obj. 9) List two ways to check whether you are using the correct format and writing style in preparing your dissertation.
Answer (any 2 OK):

    a.   Obtain a copy of the style manual approved by your institution for preparing dissertations.

    b.   Ask your dissertation chairperson to identify several outstanding dissertations completed at your institution that you can examine.

    c. If you hire someone to type your dissertation, check whether he is familiar with the format requirements of your institution.

12. (obj. 9) List two of the topics that the discussion chapter of a dissertation should cover.
Answer (any 2 OK):

    a.   A brief restatement of the research problem investigated and of the method used to study it.

    b.   An interpretation of each major finding.

    c.   A discussion of the methodological limitations of the study.

    d.   A summary of the implications of the findings for practice.

    e.   Possible questions that could be addressed in further research.

13. (obj. 10) Name two factors to consider in deciding on a journal to which to submit a report of your research study.

Answer (any 2 OK):

    a. Identification of a journal that is most likely to publish studies on the problem that you investigated.

    b. The journal's reputation, i.e., how widely read and influential it appears to be.

    c. Whether it is a refereed journal.

14. (obj. 11)

Give one reason why a chart essay is a desirable format for presenting a paper at a professional meeting.

Answer (any 1 OK):

    a. The chart essay simplifies the elements of a research study by using charts to focus the audience's attention on aspects of the study that are most relevant to policy making.

    b. The chart essay makes the study more understandable to policy makers or practitioners, who have less familiarity with research methodology than most researchers.

APPLICATION PROBLEMS

Problem 1

a. State three of your areas of interest in education.

b. Mention two problems in each of these areas that you think are worthy of research investigation.

c. Write (1) a null hypothesis, (2) a directional hypothesis, and (3) a research objective for one of the problems you mentioned.

Sample Answer:

a. Three Areas of Interest

   (1) Evaluation of teaching effectiveness.

   (2) Teacher supervision.

   (3) Creativity.

b. Two Problems in Each Area

   (1) Development of classroom observation systems; The relationship between particular teaching techniques and student outcomes.

   (2) Characteristics of effective supervisors; Typical interaction patterns between supervisors and teachers.

   (3) Development of techniques for increasing creativity; School achievement of creative children.

c. For the Problem of the Relationship between Particular Teaching Techniques and Student Outcomes

   (1) Sample null hypothesis: Mathematics teachers who use specific feedback during math lessons and comparable teachers who use general feedback do not obtain different levels of student gain in mathematics achievement.

   (2) Sample directional hypothesis: Mathematics teachers who use specific feedback during math lessons obtain higher student achievement gains than comparable teachers who use general feedback.

   (3) Sample objective: The objective of this study is to determine whether there is a difference in mathematics achievement for the students of mathematics teachers who use specific feedback compared with those who use general feedback.

Problem 2

A graduate student claims that it is not necessary for her to do a pilot study prior to conducting an experiment for her doctoral dissertation. Her experiment is primarily a replication of a previously published study on the effectiveness of a teacher inservice on classroom management, with a few modifications. Give at least two arguments in favor of her doing a pilot study under these conditions.

Sample Answer (any 2 OK):

    a.   The pilot study may help her develop new hypotheses to be tested about the effects of the classroom management inservice.

    b.   It may help her discover problems with teachers' application of what they learned that were not mentioned in the report of the previous study.

    c.   It may help her discover new classroom management procedures that are more effective than those that were tested in the previous study.

    d.   It provides a test of the modifications in the teacher inservice procedures that she has made to those in the previous study.

Problem 3

Rewrite the following dissertation titles so that they are brief yet informative.

    a.   "A Study Investigating the Relationship between Selected Personality Factors in First-, Second-, and Third-Grade Children and their Attitudes toward School at Various Intervals in the School Year."

    b.   "A Preliminary Investigation into the Effects of Participation in a High School Counseling Program on Student Perceptions of Various Aspects of College."

Sample Answer:

    a.   "The Relationship between Personality and Attitudes Toward School in Primary-Grade Children."

    b.   "Effects of a High School Counseling Program on Student Perceptions of College."

TEACHING ACTIVITIES

Activity 1

Give students several statements of research problems (e.g., the effects of parental involvement on the homework completion of primary-grade students). Ask each student to write a hypothesis, a research question, and a research objective for a research study that could be generated from the problem statement. Discuss the students' work in class, noting strengths and weaknesses of selected hypotheses, questions, and objectives.

Activity 2
Bring a research proposal to class that has been reviewed by a local institutional review board. Have students in groups evaluate the strengths and weaknesses of each section, and make recommendations to correct weaknesses. If possible, compare their comments to those made by the institutional review board.

Activity 3
Bring a clear, detailed abstract or summary of a research report to class, along with copies of three journals that you think are good candidates to which to submit the research report. Have students in groups examine the publication guidelines of each of the journals. Then have them discuss the pros and cons of submitting the report of the completed study to each of the journals and how the report might differ depending on which journal it was submitted to.

Activity 4
Have students review a program listing the presentations at a meeting of the American Educational Research Association or another major association. Ask them to find several presentations that appear relevant to the research problem they wish to investigate. In class, have students discuss why the presentations they selected might be relevant and what they might learn by actually attending them.

CHAPTER 3
ETHICAL, LEGAL, AND HUMAN RELATIONS ISSUES
IN EDUCATIONAL RESEARCH

Note: The phrase in parentheses following the item number for both closed-form and open-form items, for example, 1. (obj. 3), refers to the textbook chapter objective to which the item is keyed.

CLOSED-FORM ITEMS

1. (obj. 1) Ethical practice requires the research investigator to
   a. protect participants from physical and mental discomfort, harm, or danger.
   b. refrain from the use of deception in any research study.
   c. develop a written contract defining the participants' obligations concerning their involvement in the study.
   d. provide access to data on individuals to other qualified researchers.
Answer: a

2. (obj. 1) Currently prevailing legal constraints on educational research include the requirement that
   a. school records on individual students will not be released under any conditions without parental consent.
   b. no unauthorized person can have access to the names of the students who participated in the study.
   c. a national government review board must approve all research projects involving human subjects.
   d. deception may not be used in experiments with children.
Answer: b

3. (obj. 2) Professional associations such as the American Educational Research Association have developed written codes of ethics primarily because
   a. many researchers have violated ethical principles.
   b. institutional review boards are required to use such codes in evaluating research proposals.
   c. public and governmental concern about the effects of research on human subjects has increased.
   d. all of the above.
Answer: c

4. (obj. 3) The main function of an institutional review board is to
   a. determine procedures for allowing institutionalized individuals to participate in research studies.
   b. review research proposals to ensure that they provide satisfactory protection of human subjects.
   c. review research proposals to ensure that the research will yield useful results for the sponsoring institution.
   d. review completed research studies to ensure that human subjects were adequately protected.

Answer: b

5. (obj. 3) Proposals for research that are defined by federal regulations as exempt from review are those that
   a. receive funds from a U.S. government agency.
   b. involve fewer than 10 subjects in each group.
   c. involve minimal risk to human subjects.
   d. will be conducted entirely within the institution that is reviewing the proposal.

Answer: c

6. (obj. 4) Match each of the following procedures that is used to protect human research subjects with the appropriate example of that procedure.
   __ 1. Describe the conditions of participants' participation in the study.
   __ 2. Ensure that participants can exercise their right to withdraw from the study at any time.
   __ 3. Protect participants' privacy and confidentiality.
   __ 4. Assess the risk-benefit ratio.
   __ 5. Apply safeguards when using deception.
      a. Asking, "Would you like to stop now?"
      b. Telling participants at the outset who will have access to the data.
      c. Explaining to participants that their behavior during the study was not unusual.
      d. Sending an informed consent letter.
      e. Doing a literature review to determine whether the proposed treatment has unanticipated side effects.

Answers: 1=d, 2=a, 3=b, 4=e, 5=c

7. (obj. 5) A major advantage of using a coding or linkage system to ensure the confidentiality of data on human subjects is that
   a. data protected by a coding or linkage system have privileged legal status in the courts.
   b. this system guarantees research participants that no one can determine how they responded to the research instruments.
   c. this approach is more ethical than a completely anonymous procedure.
   d. if necessary, the researcher can identify participants who failed to respond or misinterpreted the instructions.

Answer: d

8. (obj. 6) A valid reason for using deception in some behavioral science research is that
   a. if participants knew the purpose of the study, they might respond differently and thus invalidate the results.
   b. some studies involve aversive experiences, and participants might refuse to participate if they knew this fact.
   c. many researchers are interested in the study of how individuals respond to the fact that they have been deceived.
   d. it increases the likelihood of significant differences between the experimental and control group subjects.

Answer: a

9. (obj. 6) It is important to dehoax subjects at the end of an experiment involving deception in order to
   a. discourage the subjects from revealing the true purpose of the experiment to other potential subjects.
   b. help ensure that the deception will do no future harm to the subjects.
   c. solicit data about the subjects' post-experiment perceptions of the deception.
   d. explain the expected findings of the experiment.

Answer: b

10. (obj. 6) Desensitizing subjects after an experiment typically involves
   a. telling them that they were in the control group rather than the experimental group.
   b. pointing out that their behavior was unpredictable.
   c. suggesting that their behavior was due to the circumstances present in the experiment.
   d. pointing out their responsibility for their own actions.

Answer: c

11. (obj. 7) Disseminating research results in the "least publishable unit" rather than as a coherent whole is unethical because
    a.   it distorts the meaning of the research.
    b.   it gives authors excessive credit for the extent of their publishable work.
    c.   it makes scarce reporting space less available to other authors.
    d.   all of the above.
Answer: d

12. (obj. 8) Which of the following is not a legitimate request for the researcher to agree to when seeking approval of a research project from school personnel?
    a.   The results will be useful to the schools in their district.
    b.   The study will contribute to the profession of education.
    c.   Any aspects of the research design that interfere with other school activities will be modified.
    d.   Minimal extra time and effort will be required from students who participate.
Answer: c

13. (obj. 8) A research project involved individual administration of a new measure of nonverbal intelligence to low-achieving children. The test identified a number of children with previously undiagnosed learning deficits. This example illustrates
    a.   the possible advantages to the school district of research that uses special measures.
    b.   the potential dangers of not ensuring anonymity of research subjects.
    c.   the importance of modifying the research design to accommodate school requirements.
    d.   the need for obtaining prior approval from school authorities for all measures to be used in the research.
Answer: a

14. (obj. 8) In research done in school settings, it generally is wise for the researcher to
    a.   get approval from the teachers who will be involved before contacting the superintendent or principal.
    b.   conceal the true purpose of the research from the teachers whose students may be involved in it.
    c.   maintain distance from school personnel in order not to bias the results.
    d.   think of ways to ensure that aspects of the study will provide direct benefits to the school.
Answer: d

OPEN-FORM ITEMS

1. (obj. 1) An investigator conducts a study of the effects of large vitamin doses on college students' problem-solving ability. When he describes the study to his philosophy class, all the students agree to participate. A week later a student tells the professor she does not want to finish the project because she feels she is taking too many vitamins. The investigator points out that the doses are well within safe limits established by the medical profession. The student still wishes to drop out. Because the student was fully informed before the study and volunteered, would it be ethical for the professor to penalize the student by giving her a lower grade in the class? Explain your answer.
Answer:
No, doing so would violate professional ethics. The professor must allow the student to withdraw from the study without penalty.

2. (obj. 2) The American Psychological Association (APA) has developed an ethics code that includes (1) general ethical standards, and standards for (2) evaluation, assessment, or intervention; (3) advertising and other public statements; (4) therapy; (5) privacy and confidentiality; (6) teaching, training, supervision, research, and publishing; (7) forensic activities; and (8) resolution of ethical issues. List two of these standards that are highly relevant to the conduct of educational research.
Answer (any 2 OK):
Standards 2, 5, 6, and 8.

3. (obj. 2) Explain how the risk-benefit ratio is used in the review of a research proposal.
Answer:
If the proposed study is likely to expose subjects to possible physical, psychological, or legal harm, the researcher must demonstrate that it provides sufficient benefits to the subjects, or to research knowledge in general, to outweigh the risk of harm to which research participants will be exposed.

4. (obj. 4) One of the steps required to protect the rights of research subjects is to give each subject a letter of informed consent. Briefly describe three types of information that such a letter should cover.

Answer (any 3 OK):

    a.   Participants are informed of the information that will be disclosed to the researchers.

    b.   The tests and experimental procedures to be used are described.

    c.   Participants are informed that they may withdraw from participation at any time.

    d.   Participants are informed that any incentives promised for participation will be received even if they withdraw from the study.

    e.   Participants are informed of the purpose of the research by the end of the study, if not sooner.

    f.   Participants are given their own copy of the informed consent letter to keep, and they are asked to return a signed copy to the researcher to signify their informed consent.

5. (obj. 5) Describe three steps that can be taken to protect the privacy of individuals who are to serve as subjects in a research project.

Answer: (any 3 OK):

    a.   Get written consent from the subjects or their guardians before accessing school records.

    b.   Use codes instead of names on measures.

    c.   Set up procedures to limit access to the data.

    d.   Do not use the data for purposes other than those originally intended without the prior consent of the subjects.

    e.   Do not share information about specific subjects with teachers or others involved in the research.

    f. Do not include the subjects' names in research reports or other documents, except with their prior consent.

6. (obj. 5) Briefly describe three strategies that can be used to maintain the confidentiality of information gathered on research subjects.

Answer (any 3 OK):

    a.   Have subjects furnish all information anonymously.

    b.   Use a third party to select the sample and collect the data.

    c.   Use an identifier that is destroyed as soon as the individual's response is received.

    d.   Have subjects make up their own code numbers or aliases.

    e.   Dispose of sensitive data after a designated time.

7. (obj. 6) The use of deception in a research study requires the researcher to ask herself several questions, such as whether the potential benefits of the study justify the use of deception. Briefly describe two other questions the researcher should consider before using deception.

Answer (any 2 OK):

    a. Do the researcher's personal ethics permit deception for any purpose?

    b. Are there alternate procedures that would not require deception?

    c. Will the deception undercut the subjects' rights to be informed about the potential risk of participation in the research?

    d. Will the use of deception cause negative effects on the subjects, such as cynicism, resentment, or loss of self-esteem?

    e. Have safeguards such as debriefing been included in the research plan to minimize potential negative outcomes?

8. (obj. 6) Some research projects require desensitization of subjects. Explain desensitization, and give an example of a type of study in which it would be necessary.

Answer:

Desensitization is the process of helping subjects deal with new information about themselves as a consequence of the behavior they exhibited during the experiment. For example, if subjects are induced to exhibit dishonest behavior or to behave cruelly toward others in a research study, desensitization would be necessary.

9. (obj. 7) Describe three unethical practices involving the reporting of research that researchers should avoid.

Answer (any 3 OK):

    a. Partial publication, i.e., disseminating research results in the "least publishable unit" in order to inflate the author's list of publications.

    b. Dual publication, i.e., publishing the same research results in more than one publication in order to inflate the author's list of publications.

    c. Plagiarism, i.e., directly lifting another's words for use in one's own publications.

    d. Paraphragiarism, i.e., closely copying another writer's words or ideas without giving credit to the original author.

    e. Not giving all persons closely involved in the research an opportunity to be listed as co-authors.

10. (obj. 8) Describe one advantage and one disadvantage of conducting one's dissertation research project at the institution where one is employed.

Answer (any 1 from each set OK):

Advantages

a. Ease of obtaining approval because of access to institutional decision makers.

b. Familiarity with the institution's routines.

c. The logistical convenience in conducting the study where one already is located.

Disadvantages

a. Less sensitivity to other members' perspectives because of one's position in the institution.

b. Vulnerability to certain sanctions because of one's employment or relationship with particular individuals.

c. Conflict between being a researcher and one's normal institutional role.

11. (obj. 8) If members of the community protest a research study, what are three things the researcher can communicate publicly to reduce possible resistance to the study?

Answer (any 3 OK):

a. Point out the procedures that were used to obtain the informed consent of research subjects.

b. Explain the steps being taken to protect the safety and confidentiality of research participants.

c. Emphasize the benefits that research participants will derive from being involved in the study.

d. Describe the positive outcomes of past studies related to your research.

APPLICATION PROBLEMS

Problem 1

You are meeting with the district superintendent to explain a research project you wish to conduct that involves giving personality tests to high school students and teachers. The superintendent asks, "What steps are you taking to protect the rights of the teachers and students who will be in your experiment?" Describe the steps that you could mention.

Sample Answer:

a. Each individual's consent will be obtained prior to the start of the project.

b. The test data will be kept confidential; names of subjects will be removed from the tests as soon as possible.

c. When the research design permits, tests will be anonymous.

d. All participants will be fully informed in advance of the conditions of their participation.

Problem 2
"Many educational practitioners do not understand the nature of educational research. Therefore, the researcher only needs to inform administrators and teachers about the general purpose of his research project. They need not be informed of specifics, such as tests to be administered, number of students to be involved, how the results will be reported, etc." Is this a sound position to take? Support your answer.

Sample Answer:

No. Educational practitioners usually want specific information about details of any research project that will affect them. For example, they will want to know who is to be involved, whether the tests are controversial, how the participants' right to privacy is to be protected, and whether the findings might reflect unfavorably on the school district.

Problem 3
The text describes three criteria that educators should consider in deciding whether to agree to have their institution participate in a research study. The criteria are (1) the conceptual soundness of the research, (2) the feasibility of the research, and (3) whether the research is ethically designed. Say that a high school has been asked to participate in research comparing a standard, in-class career education unit with an innovative program in which students are placed in work sites for part of the school day. Give an example of a concern that might arise in relation to each criterion.

Sample Answer:

a. Are the work sites ones in which students can learn skills and concepts of value rather than simply putting in time?

b. Will it be possible for students to satisfy course requirements for graduation while also working during the day?

c. Will employers provide training, pay, or other incentives instead of simply leaving students on their own?

Problem 4

In a study of truthfulness, you set up research conditions that make it possible to detect certain lies that subjects are likely to make, which could not be detected under normal conditions. At the end of the study, several participants appear to be very upset when they discover that they have been caught in lies. As the investigator, suggest the steps you could take to meet your responsibility to the research participants.

Sample Answer:

The investigator should take steps to ensure the adequate desensitization of subjects, including the following:

    a.   Do not conduct the study until you have planned a desensitization procedure and tried it out in a small-scale pilot study.

    b.   Point out that most people tell a great many small lies in situations in which they believe there is no chance to be caught.

    c.   Provide evidence to support the statement in (b) above, if possible. This could include data from previous research as well as the research in question.

    d.   Check on whether all participants have accepted your arguments. If not, arrange individual conferences and, if necessary, counseling, for participants who still appear to be troubled.

Problem 5

Suppose you have carried out a study in which you gave students incorrect scores on a test of algebra aptitude (some higher and some lower than the correct scores) to see how this information affects responses on a vocational interest test to vocations that require mathematics (e.g., electrical engineering and computer programming). Describe the procedure you would use to debrief students at the completion of the study.

Sample Answer:

Incorrect scores on this test could lead students to develop incorrect self perceptions and aspirations. Therefore, the investigator should use a procedure to dehoax students at the end of the study. This procedure could include the following steps:

    a.   Describe the purpose of the study and explain why the deception was necessary.

    b.   Hold individual conferences with the students to show them their test papers, point out their correct score, and discuss how this score was changed.

    c.   Give students a questionnaire to determine if they are dehoaxed, i.e., do they believe your explanation and accept their actual score on the test?

    d.   Offer to give students another algebra aptitude test so they can be sure of their actual performance.

TEACHING ACTIVITIES

Activity 1
Obtain a research proposal and copies of comments made by the institutional review board that reviewed it. Ask your students to review the ethical strengths and weaknesses of the proposal. Compare the students' comments with those of the IRB.

Activity 2
Identify a real or simulated proposal for a research study. Ask students to generate a list of points that should be included in a letter of informed consent to potential participants in this study.

Activity 3
Invite someone who is serving on an institutional review board to your class. The discussion can focus on ethical issues that have come up before the board. Also, students can ask the board member questions about potential ethical problems in the research studies that they are planning to do.

Activity 4
Invite to class a researcher who is conducting an ongoing study in a field setting. Ask the researcher to speak about the procedures that she used to protect human subjects, her experiences with an institutional review board, and any human relations issues that arose in the field setting and their resolution.

Activity 5
Ask students to bring to class a list of one ethical standard, one legal requirement, and one human relations principle that is particularly relevant to the research they propose to do for their master's thesis or doctoral dissertation. Discuss examples of each.

CHAPTER 4
REVIEWING THE LITERATURE

Note: The phrase in parentheses following the item number for both closed-form and open-form items, for example, 1. (obj. 3), refers to the textbook chapter objective to which the item is keyed.

CLOSED-FORM ITEMS

1. (obj. 1) A researcher wishes to explore differences in children's conceptions of learning related to their gender and social class. In what situation should the researcher collect data *before* reviewing the literature?
   a. The researcher intends to develop grounded theory about how social class and gender affect children's conceptions of learning.
   b. The researcher intends to develop a new measure of conceptions of learning.
   c. The researcher plans to study a population of children that he thinks has not been studied previously.
   d. The researcher plans to test hypotheses derived from a theory of intellectual development.

Answer: a

2. (obj. 1) Match the following purposes of a literature review with the example that illustrates that purpose.
   ___ 1. Delimiting the research problem.
   ___ 2. Seeking new lines of inquiry.
   ___ 3. Avoiding fruitless approaches.
   ___ 4. Gaining methodological insights.
   ___ 5. Identifying recommendations for further research.
   ___ 6. Seeking support for grounded theory.
       a. A researcher identifies attempted programs that were unsuccessful in reducing dropout rates.
       b. A researcher explores suggestions that other researchers have posed to determine the best ways to keep students in school until graduation.
       c. A researcher identifies all the major lines of inquiry that have been pursued in the field of dropout prevention.
       d. A researcher develops a conceptual model to explain why students tend to leave school at key transition points during their school years.
       e. A researcher speculates about the possible value of an approach to dropout prevention that has not been previously tried.
       f. A researcher examines the findings concerning an established dropout prevention program to identify the types of students for whom the program was most successful.

Answers: 1=c, 2=e, 3=a, 4=f, 5=b, 6=d

3. (obj. 1) It is important to conduct a review of literature before starting a research project in order to
   a. gain insight into the research methods used by other investigators.
   b. select tried-and-true approaches.
   c. broaden the research problem.
   d. compare preliminary sources.

Answer: a

4. (obj. 2) A good first step in conducting a literature review for a research study is to
   a. finalize your problem statement before reading any primary sources.
   b. do a thorough search of each preliminary source that indexes the literature relevant to your problem.
   c. read selected secondary sources to get an overview of the literature relevant to your problem.
   d. read the references in various primary sources to generate a list of other primary sources.

Answer: c

5. (obj. 3) A drawback of using secondary sources in reviews of the research literature is that
    a. for many topics in education, primary sources are more accessible.
    b. changes and omissions may have been made in the description of the original studies.
    c. it takes longer to obtain an overview of a topic when using secondary sources.
    d. the number of secondary sources in education and the social sciences is very limited.
Answer: b

6. (obj. 3) Mark a *P* in front of the sources listed below that most likely are primary sources and an *S* in front of those that most likely are secondary sources.
    __ a.   A textbook on educational research.
    __ b.   An annual review of literature on an educational topic.
    __ c.   An article describing the author's dissertation investigation.
    __ d.   A final report of the results of an evaluation study.
    __ e.   An encyclopedia article about educational research methods.
    __ f.   A summary of the findings of several experiments that the author helped conduct.
Answer: a=S, b=S, c=P, d=P, e=S, f=P

7. (obj. 3) In educational research, the review of the literature should concentrate on presenting information from ___ sources.
    a. primary
    b. secondary
    c. preliminary
    d. theoretical
Answer: a

8. (obj. 4) In a literature review, computers are most useful for
    a. evaluating the accessibility of primary source documents.
    b. checking preliminary sources.
    c. reading the text of selected references.
    d. synthesizing primary source findings.
Answer: b

9. (obj. 4) The *Thesaurus of ERIC Descriptors* is particularly useful for
    a. determining preliminary sources that have indexed literature related to your problem.
    b. identifying key terms to use in searching for relevant citations.
    c. identifying sources of fugitive literature.
    d. all of the above.
Answer: b

10. (obj. •) The ERIC clearinghouses are responsible for
    a. evaluating the quality of research reports to determine whether they merit being indexed in ERIC.
    b. preparing hard copies of primary source documents for users.
    c. conducting computer searches for users on defined problems relevant to each clearinghouse's focus.
    d. cataloging and abstracting documents in particular subject areas.

Answer: d

11. (obj. 4) In doing a hard-copy search of the *Current Index to Journals in Education* (*CIJE*) on the topic of providing education to unwed mothers, it is wise for the researcher to
    a. identify main-entry descriptors in the *Thesaurus of ERIC Descriptors* that correspond to the terms most relevant to this topic.
    b. include as descriptors all the terms listed in the *Thesaurus of ERIC Descriptors* as being related to each relevant main-entry descriptor.
    c. use a narrower term as one's main-entry descriptor, if possible.
    d. use only descriptors for which there are a substantial number of citations indexed in *CIJE*.

Answer: a

12. (obj. 4) A disadvantage of the use of a CD-ROM version of *Resources in Education* compared to its hard-copy version is that the user
    a. must use approved descriptors to search the CD-ROM version.
    b. cannot start a search by identifying the documents written by a selected author.
    c. may not be able to obtain the most recent citations.
    d. usually must pay a fee to use a library's CD-ROM version.

Answer: c

13 (obj. 4) The best way to locate the publications of a specific author when searching the *Current Index to Journals in Education* by computer is to
    a. search free text for terms contained anywhere in the citation.
    b. search the index for all variants of the author's name.
    c. search the thesaurus for approved ERIC descriptors.
    d. combine the author's name with your primary topic descriptors using an *and* connector.

Answer: b

14. (obj. 4) The best way to locate all the citations involving anything having to do with parents when searching ERIC is to enter ___ in your computer search.
    a. the term *parent*
    b. the term *parenting*
    c. the term *parent**
    d. all three of the above terms connected by *or*

Answer: c

15. (obj. 5) The feature of the ERIC preliminary sources that probably is most helpful to educational researchers is its
    a. being funded through library user fees.
    b   ongoing publication of a hard-copy version.
    c. monthly updating of the CD-ROM version.
    d. extensive coverage of a wide variety of educational documents.

Answer: d

16. (obj. 6) A major advantage of the Internet over other computer search procedures for researchers is its
    a. low cost.
    b. speed in providing the requested information.
    c. inventory of secondary sources on educational topics.
    d. provision of access to thousands of research-related databases.

Answer: d

17. (obj. 6) Match each capability of the Internet with the appropriate example of how this capability could help an educational researcher who is doing a literature search for a proposed study on strategies to increase parent involvement in children's learning efforts.

___ 1. Searching preliminary sources and other databases.
___ 2. Electronic mail (e-mail).
___ 3. Electronic bulletin boards.
___ 4. Electronic journals.
___ 5. File transfer.

    a. The researcher could send a message to another researcher who has done research on parenting.
    b. The researcher could access and read complete research reports about school policies in relation to parent involvement.
    c. The researcher could obtain demographic statistical data about parents and families.
    d. The researcher could request information from other Internet users about any upcoming conferences about parent involvement.
    e. The researcher could send drafts of his research proposal for review by researchers at several institutions.

Answers: 1=c, 2=a, 3=d, 4=b, 5=e

18. (obj. 7) Reading a secondary source on the topic of research about class size is of particular benefit to a researcher planning to carry out a study involving this variable because
    a. it provides the direct perspective of the individuals who conducted the research.
    b. it combines knowledge from many primary sources into a single publication.
    c. it provides an exhaustive list of primary sources relevant to the topic of class size.
    d. it eliminates the need to do one's own synthesis of the primary source literature.

Answer: b

19. (obj. 8) Meta-analysis involves
    a. the search for theoretical concepts or themes in a set of quantitative and qualitative research studies that investigated the same topic.
    b. the exclusion of studies reporting nonsignificant findings from a review of research on a topic.
    c. a search for trends in the effect sizes among the findings of a set of quantitative research studies that investigated the same topic.
    d. a qualitative analysis of the practical significance of an accumulation of statistical findings concerning a research topic.

Answer: c

20. (obj. 9) WORLDCAT is an electronic
   a.   database of primary source documents.
   b.   database of secondary source documents.
   c.   index to journal articles in education.
   d.   index to books and journals in many different libraries.

Answer: d

21. (obj. 10) The best basis for classifying primary source documents in preparation for writing a literature review usually is by
   a.   the question, objective or hypothesis in one's study to which the document pertains.
   b.   a code classifying each document as primarily concerned with research, theory, or opinion.
   c.   the year of publication.
   d.   the quality of the study's methodology.

Answer: a

22. (obj. 11) Studies of the perceived quality of published educational research reports suggest that
   a.   about half the studies that appear should not have been published in their present form.
   b.   the writer of a research report should be the ultimate judge of the report's quality.
   c.   evaluating research reports for quality is beyond the capability of most educational researchers.
   d.   the vast majority of published studies are of high quality.

Answer: a

23. (obj. 12) In writing a literature review, a researcher begins by devoting a paragraph to each study, in which he lists the authors, describes the measures and treatments used, and indicates the significance level of the findings. This type of literature review appears to have the following flaw:
   a.   failing to describe the search procedure by which he identified the sources reviewed.
   b.   not considering the soundness of the methodology used to generate the findings.
   c.   not fitting the findings into a conceptual or theoretical framework.
   d.   all of the above.

Answer: d

24. (obj. 13) Match each method of synthesizing the findings of a literature review listed below with the appropriate characteristic of that method.

  __ 1.   Narrative review.
  __ 2.   Vote-counting.
  __ 3.   Chi-square method.
  __ 4.   Meta-analysis.

    a.   Calculates a statistic called *effect size* to assess the overall magnitude of the statistical significance of the findings obtained in every available study on a given topic.
    b.   Cumulates data on the probability values that were obtained in a set of studies on a given topic.
    c.   Provides a subjective summary of selected research, theory, and opinion related to a topic.
    d.   Classifies studies included in the review into categories based on the direction and statistical significance of the findings.

Answers: 1=c, 2=d, 3=b, 4=a

25. (obj. 13) The most serious shortcoming of a narrative literature review is that
    a. insufficient attention is given to the better studies.
    b. this type of review does not provide a quantitative estimate of the treatment effect or the degree of the relationship between variables in each of the reviewed studies.
    c. the statistical significance of each t or F value in the primary sources is ignored.
    d. this approach overlooks the qualitative aspects of the research reviewed.

Answer: b

26. (obj. 13) An advantage of the vote-counting method of synthesizing related research studies is that it
    a. eliminates the need to consider the statistical significance of the findings.
    b. includes only the statistically significant studies.
    c. is much less likely to produce misleading results than other methods.
    d. requires less information about the individual studies than other methods.

Answer: d

27. (obj. 13) The most persistent criticism of meta-analysis as a method of reviewing research literature is that
- a. there is no way to determine the significance of the combined results.
- b. only one finding from each study can be included even if several significant results are reported.
- c. the review includes data from studies that were poorly designed and executed.
- d. the calculation of effect sizes is subject to researcher bias.

Answer: c

28. (obj. 14) In using Ogawa and Malen's approach to synthesizing qualitative research studies that is based on the principles and procedures of the exploratory case study method, the reviewer
- a. attempts to reach strong conclusions about the effects of the intervention that was studied.
- b. should avoid using explicit definitions of constructs to guide the review process.
- c. can include quantitative research reports as part of the literature to be reviewed.
- d. should not speculate about causal patterns in the cases included in the literature review.

Answer: c

OPEN-FORM ITEMS

1. (obj. 1) Say that you plan to do research that involves designing and evaluating a high school course about career planning. Describe two purposes of doing a literature review concerning your topic.
Answer (any 2 OK):

   a. To determine the various types of programs that have been designed to teach students about careers.

   b. To identify promising new ways in which students can be helped to explore possible careers.

   c. To choose teaching strategies for the course that have been successful and avoid those that have been unsuccessful.

   d. To design an evaluation of the course that will allows its effectiveness to be tested in a sound manner.

   e. To build on the experiences of other researchers who have taught or evaluated similar courses.

   f. To build grounded theory about how students develop their conceptions of their own and others' potential careers.

2. (obj. 2) Describe two of the steps that should be included in a thorough review of the literature after you have defined your research problem and identified key terms related to the problem.

Answer (any 2 OK):

a. Search preliminary sources that index the literature relevant to your problem.

b. Identify and read secondary sources that review the literature relevant to your problem.

c. Obtain and read the primary sources that bear most closely on your research problem.

d. Write a synthesis of what you have learned from the secondary and primary sources you have read.

3. (obj. 3)

a. What type of source of the educational literature is most similar to the subject index of a typical library catalog?

b. Name two ways in which this source differs from a library catalog.

Answer:

a. A preliminary source is similar to the subject index of a library catalog, because it indexes particular bodies of literature relevant to a given subject.

b. A preliminary source differs from a library catalog in two ways: (1) A preliminary source indexes all sorts of publications, whereas a library catalog indexes only books. (2) A preliminary source includes publications wherever they may be located, whereas a library catalog lists only the holdings of a particular library.

4. (obj. 3) Define the terms (a) *preliminary source,* (b) *secondary source,* and (c) *primary source.*

Answer:

a. A preliminary source indexes particular bodies of literature relevant to various topics.

b. A secondary source is written by someone who did not actually do the research, develop the theories, or express the opinions that are presented, but that reviews and summarizes the research, theories, or opinions of others.

c. A primary source is an original report written by the individuals who actually conducted the research, developed the theory, or formulated the opinions that are described.

5. (obj. 3)
    a.   Describe the difference between a primary and a secondary source.
    b.   Give an example of a source of each type that deals with the topic of student achievement.
Answer:
    a.   The key difference is whether the reporter personally observed or participated in the events reported (a primary source) or did not observe or participate in the events reported (a secondary source).
    b.   An example of a primary source is an article, written by the researcher and published in a research journal, that describes an experiment conducted by the researcher to raise student achievement through increased teacher praise. An example of a secondary source is an encyclopedia article describing various ways of defining and measuring student achievement and presenting highlights from other investigators' research studies about the effects of various interventions on student achievement.

6. (obj. 3) Suppose that you have located a very controversial article related to your area of interest.
    a.   What is the best source you could use to locate subsequent articles that challenge or support the positions stated in the original article?
    b.   How would you use this source?
Answer:
    a.   The author section of the *Social Science Citation Index*.
    b.   Look up the author of the original article and find out who has cited this article. Some of the people who have cited the article would state strong pro or con positions.

7. (obj. 4) Name two types of information about a document that typically are included in an ERIC citation.
Answer (any 2 OK):
    a.   The authors.
    b.   The title.
    c.   The year of publication.
    d.   The publisher.

8. (obj. 4) What is the effect of using *or* connectors and *and* connectors on the number of citations retrieved by a computer search?
Answer:
Or connectors tend to increase the number of citations selected, because any citation is selected that has either of the descriptors that are connected by *or*. *And* connectors tend to decrease the number of citations selected, because any reference selected must include both of the descriptors that are connected by *and*.

9. (obj. 4) When searching a preliminary source like *CIJE* for citations related to several major concepts, such as "the relationship between *locus-of-control, achievement,* and *attitudes toward school* among *high school students,*" describe one advantage of a computer search over a manual search.
Answer (any 1 OK):

    a.   The computer can simultaneously search for citations that have descriptors related to all the major concepts in the research problem.

    b.   The computer search is much less time-consuming.

    c.   The computer search provides a convenient printout of the citations relevant to one's research problem.

10. (obj. 4) Suppose you conduct an ERIC computer search using the descriptors *faculty workload, teacher burnout,* and *secondary education,* and you locate only a few relevant citations. Name one way you could broaden your search to identify more citations.
Answer (any 1 OK):

    a.   For each concept, add related terms (RT) from the ERIC *Thesaurus* and link them with *or* connectors.

    b.   Eliminate the third descriptor, *secondary education,* so that you will obtain citations relevant to any educational level.

11. (obj. 4) Define proximity searching, and name two conditions when it is most useful.
Answer:

Proximity searching is a computer procedure used to search for citations containing words or phrases that occur in proximity to (i.e., next to) each other. It is most useful when (a) there are no descriptor terms that fit your topic precisely, and (b) you wish to search a very narrow and sharply defined topic.

12. (obj. 5) Describe two types of information that are indexed by preliminary sources other than *CIJE* and *RIE* which an educational researcher might wish to examine in carrying out a literature search.
Answer (any 2 OK):
  a. Bibliographies.
  b. Book reviews.
  c. Books in education and related fields.
  d. Curriculum materials.
  e. Directories.
  f. Dissertations and theses.
  g. Journal articles, papers, and reports that are related to education but are not indexed by *CIJE*.
  h. Magazines and newspapers.
  i. Tests and self-report measures.

13. (obj. 6) Describe two of the present capabilities of the Internet.
Answer (any 2 OK):
  a. You can search preliminary sources and other databases not locally available.
  b. You can personally communicate by electronic mail (e-mail) with another Internet user.
  c. You can post standard messages to Internet users with common interests on an electronic bulletin board.
  d. You can send computer files to, or receive files from, other Internet users.

14. (obj. 6) Describe one advantage of an electronic journal of educational research.
Answer (any 1 OK):
  a. It saves institutions the time and expense of buying, cataloging, storing, and managing access to traditional hard-copy journal issues.
  b. It saves users the time and expense of locating and copying journal articles at the library or of subscribing to a journal directly.
  c. Reports of research are available to readers soon after they are completed, instead of after a delay of many months until publication in hard-copy form.

15. (obj. 7) Name one standard secondary source that is a particularly good source of reviews on a variety of current topics of interest to many educational researchers.
Answer (any 1 OK):
  a. The yearbook *Review of Research in Education.*
  b. The *International Encyclopedia of Education.*
  c. The *Encyclopedia of Educational Research.*
  d. The journal *Review of Educational Research.*

16. (obj. 8). For a review of research on a given topic, describe one benefit of reading a meta-analysis compared to a standard encyclopedia article.
Answer (any 1 OK):

    a.   A meta-analysis directly compares the magnitude of the effects observed in different research studies on the topic.

    b.   A meta-analysis usually relates different features of specific studies to observed effect sizes.

    c.   A meta-analysis typically includes a table summarizing the design features of each study included in the meta-analysis and the magnitude of effect sizes found in the study.

17. (obj. 9) Suggest one way to obtain copies of primary source articles that are not available in your institution's library.
Answer (any 1 OK):

    a.   Contact the author to request a reprint of the article.

    b.   Order the article from a reprint service.

    c.   Locate another library that has the journal containing the article, and request that they send you a copy.

18. (obj. 10) Describe one advantage of using a coding system to classify the primary sources you identify in your literature search.
Answer (any 1 OK):

    a.   The necessity of coding each source motivates you to read it thoroughly.

    b.   The necessity of coding each source stimulates you to assess its relevance to the major topics that underlie your research problem.

    c.   Checking the codes that you have assigned will help you quickly identify the sources that are relevant to the particular topic you are addressing in each section of your literature review.

19. (obj. 11) State one question that you can pose in evaluating the quality of each of the following sections of a research report: the introduction, the research procedures, the research results, and the discussion of results.
Answer:

(See figure 4.9 in the textbook for appropriate answers to this question; any one question from each section of figure 4.9 is OK. Also see appendix F, "Questions for Evaluating Quantitative Research Reports," and appendix G, "Questions for Evaluating Qualitative Research Reports," for other relevant questions.)

20. (obj. 12) Describe one type of source that you can examine as a model in writing your literature review.

Answer (any 1 OK):

    a. Exemplary literature reviews, such as those in the *Review of Educational Research* or other high-quality secondary sources.

    b. The literature review sections of research articles and dissertations recommended to you as exemplary.

21. (obj. 12) Describe one desirable approach to conducting a review of the research literature on a particular topic.

Answer (any 1 OK):

    a. Aim toward the goal of clearly showing how the work of other researchers and theorists relates to the study being reported.

    b. Provide a description of the search procedure you used to identify the sources you discuss.

    c. Report not only on the research findings in each study you review but also on the soundness of the methodology used to generate those findings.

    d. Fit the findings, opinions, and ideas that you report into a conceptual or theoretical framework.

22. (obj. 13) Explain (a) the way in which a meta-analysis is conducted to synthesize the literature on a given topic, and (b) the main criticism of this method.

Answer:

    a. Meta-analysis is a statistical procedure for combining the results of quantitative research studies in order to make an overall estimate of the relationship between two or more variables that were investigated in these studies. An effect size is computed from the findings of each study and these effect sizes are averaged in order to estimate the overall magnitude of the relationships between the variables.

    b. The main criticism of meta-analysis is that data from poorly designed studies are included and given equal weight to data from well-designed studies.

23. (obj. 14)

    a. Define the term *audit trail* as used in a review of qualitative research literature.

    b. Describe the purpose of creating an audit trail.

Answer:

    a. An audit trail describes all the procedures and decision rules that were used by the reviewer in reviewing the literature.

    b. The purpose of creating an audit trail is to help readers to understand how the review was designed and carried out, and to replicate it if they desire to do so.

APPLICATION PROBLEMS

Problem 1

Suppose that you have identified the following research study as a useful foundation on which to build your own study: Armbruster, B. B., Anderson, T. H., & Meyer, J. L. (1991). Improving content area reading using instructional graphics. *Reading Research Quarterly*, *26*, 393-416. How can you find other published studies that refer to or build on this study?

Sample Answer:

   a.   List key terms in the abstract or introduction section of the article, check them in the *Thesaurus of ERIC Descriptors*, and do a computer search of the ERIC *Thesaurus* using the terms that are main-entry descriptors. Possible terms include: *social studies, reading, framing,* and *collaborative research*.

   b.   Using the index, do a computer search of ERIC by entering the names of each author (armbruster-b, anderson-t, and meyer-j) and entering py > 1991 to identify more recent citations by these authors.

   c.   Check recent issues of the *Social Science Citation Index* to locate citations to the work of these authors.

Problem 2

Suppose that you want to conduct a manual search of the research literature related to the effect of praise on the sharing behavior of young children.

Using the *Thesaurus of ERIC Descriptors*, list key descriptors you could use in checking issues of *RIE* and *CIJE*. Check *Psychological Abstracts* and copy the citation, in APA format, for one article that appears relevant to this topic.

Sample Answer:

Positive reinforcement, reinforcement, social reinforcement, rewards.

Barton, E. J. (1981). Developing sharing: An analysis of modeling and other behavioral techniques. *Behavior Modification*, 1981, *5*, 386-398. Several other articles related to this topic also can be found in the 1982 to 1988 *Psychological Abstracts*; see, for example, abstracts 1090 and 7530.

Problem 3

If your students have access to the Internet, you can give them the assignment of subscribing to one of the AERA bulletin boards. Subscription information is on page 141 of the textbook. You can allow students either to select their own bulletin board or designate it. AERA-GSL (Graduate Students List) might be particularly appropriate. To check that they have subscribed correctly, you can ask students to print one or more bulletin-board messages and submit the messages to you as a homework assignment.

TEACHING ACTIVITIES

Activity 1
Arrange a field trip to your institution's library, or an in-class presentation, to demonstrate the library's resources for doing a literature search and retrieving documents. Demonstrate the use of ERIC (preferably the computer version) to search the literature, having students contribute research topics and related descriptors. Give students a handout listing the other preliminary sources available at your library that are relevant to educational research (e.g., *Psychological Abstracts* or *PsycINFO*) and any guidelines for using them (e.g., hours of operation).

Activity 2
You can ask students to select and read an article in a major secondary source such as the *Encyclopedia of Educational Research* or the *International Encyclopedia of Education*, on a topic of their choice. The students can be asked to give brief oral reports in class about their articles. They might focus their oral reports on how the article would be of help to them if they were to plan a research study on the topic that they chose.

Activity 3
The concept of an effect size in a meta-analysis may be new to your students. If so, you can explain this concept in class by showing a table of effect sizes from a meta-analysis, such as the one on pages 145-146 of the textbook. You can explain how the table is constructed and also how an effect size is calculated (see pages 194-196 of the textbook).

CHAPTER 5
STATISTICAL TECHNIQUES

Note: The phrase in parentheses following the item number for both closed-form and open-form items, for example, 1. (obj. 3), refers to the textbook chapter objective to which the item is keyed.

CLOSED-FORM ITEMS

1. (obj. 1) Qualitative researchers differ from quantitative researchers in that they
   a. can specify the one best statistical technique for analyzing a given set of data.
   b. do not use descriptive statistics to represent what is happening in a situation.
   c. use statistical analysis as a supplement to interpretive analysis.
   d. all of the above.

Answer: c

2. (obj. 2) Match each type of score named below with the appropriate example.
   __ 1. High-anxiety, moderate anxiety, and low-anxiety subjects.
   __ 2. High school graduation standing.
   __ 3. Verbal IQ = 120.
   __ 4. High-anxiety and low-anxiety subjects.
   a. artificial dichotomy.
   b. categories.
   c. rank score.
   d. continuous score.
   e. true dichotomy.

Answer: 1=b, 2=c, 3=d, 4=a

3. (obj. 2) An example of a true dichotomy is
   a. male and female students.
   b. underachieving and overachieving students.
   c. percentage of students passing or failing a course.
   d. high school graduates and high school dropouts.

Answer: a

4. (obj. 2) Age equivalents, grade equivalents, and normal curve equivalent scores all are
    a. test statistics.
    b. standard scores.
    c. derived scores.
    d. all of the above.
Answer: c

5. (obj. 3) Match each statistic named below with the type of descriptive statistic under which it is classified.
    __ 1. Standard deviation
    __ 2. Bivariate coefficient.
    __ 3. Median.
    __ 4. Variance.
        a. measures of central tendency
        b. measures of variability
        c. correlational statistics
Answer: 1=b, 2=c, 3=a, 4=b

6. (obj. 4) The median of a group of scores
    a. is a measure of variability.
    b. reflects average performance less accurately than the mean when the distribution of scores is skewed.
    c. is the middle score in the distribution of scores.
    d. is an inferential statistic.
Answer: c

7. (obj. 4) Compared to the median, the mean
    a. is less stable.
    b. is more useful in analyses involving inferential statistics.
    c. provides a more accurate representation of average performance.
    d. is easier to compute.
Answer: b

8. (obj. 5) The mean and the ___ , taken together, give a good description of the nature of the group being studied.
    a. percentile distribution
    b. median
    c. standard deviation
    d. score range
Answer: c

9. (obj. 5) If a score distribution forms a normal curve,
    a. each standard deviation above or below the mean will include a fixed percentage of scores.
    b. the standard deviation can be calculated from the mean alone.
    c. the median is a better measure of central tendency than the mean.
    d. the mode is a better measure of central tendency than the median.
Answer: a

10. (obj. 6) Compared with using a *p* value of .05, using a *p* value of .01
    a. provides a more stringent test of the research hypothesis.
    b. makes a Type 1 error less likely.
    c. increases the likelihood of accepting the null hypothesis when there is a real population difference.
    d. all of the above.
Answer: d

11. (obj. 6) A significance level of .05 means that there is one chance out of ___ that the researcher will reject the null hypothesis when it is true.
    a. 100
    b. 50
    c. 10
    d. 20
Answer: d

12. (obj. 6) A test of the statistical significance of the difference between two sample means results in a *t* value that is significant at the .01 level. Which of the following is *not* a correct interpretation of this finding?
    a. The probability is 99 percent that the samples were not drawn from the same population.
    b. The mean difference exceeds the mean difference we would find once in 100 samples if the population mean difference was zero.
    c   The null hypothesis can be rejected.
    d. It is probable that the difference between the sample means reflects a true difference between the population means.
Answer: a

13. (obj. 6) When we plan a research project, we decide on the level of statistical significance we will use to reject the null hypothesis. This level is called the
    a. probability value.
    b. t level.
    c. alpha level.
    d. Type I value.
Answer: c

14. (obj. 7) One way to increase statistical power is to
    a. select a p value of .01 instead of .05.
    b. select a larger sample.
    c. decrease the risk of making a Type 1 error.
    d. use a two-tailed test of statistical significance rather than a one-tailed test.
Answer: b

15. (obj. 7) Statistical power is
    a. the power of a particular statistical test to detect a significant difference or other effect.
    b. the ratio between the significance level and the effect size.
    c. equivalent to the number of subjects included in the research study.
    d. the probability that a particular statistical test will lead to rejection of the null hypothesis.
Answer: d

16. (obj. 8) The mean and standard deviation of a sample's score distribution can be used to estimate
    a. a range of values that is likely to include the true population mean.
    b. the probability that the sample and population means truly differ.
    c. the margin of error to be expected in an individual's predicted score based on her score on the predictor measure.
    d. the mean and standard deviation of the population's score distribution.
Answer: a

17. (obj. 8) Match each example of replication below with the type of replication it illustrates.

__ 1.   The original investigator runs additional subjects through the experimental procedure.

__ 2.   After the original investigator finds a relationship between a particular measure of test anxiety and intellectual performance, another researcher develops a new measure of test anxiety and investigates the correlation between this measure and intellectual performance.

__ 3.   A researcher follows exactly the sampling and experimental procedures described in a colleague's dissertation study.

a.   Constructive replication.
b.   Literal replication.
c.   Operational replication.

Answer: 1=b, 2=a, 3=c

18. (obj. 8) A comparison of the mean scores of two groups on a test yields an effect size (ES) of 1.41. An ES of this magnitude means that

a.   the difference between the mean scores of the two groups is trivial.
b.   the difference between the mean scores of the two groups is large.
c.   the difference between the standard deviations of the two groups is trivial.
d.   both a and c above are correct.

Answer: b

19. (obj. 9) One of the advantages of stem-and-leaf displays of data is that they facilitate the detection of outliers. What is an outlier?

a.   The individual with the highest score on each leaf of the display.
b.   An individual whose score differs substantially from the other scores on any of the leaves of the display.
c.   An individual whose score is either at the top or at the bottom of the display's stem.
d.   An individual who is outside of the target population.

Answer: b

20. (obj. 10) The best approach for dealing with the problem of missing data is to

a.   have the same person carry out all aspects of the data analysis.
b.   increase the number of required data collection sessions.
c.   eliminate incomplete cases from the statistical analysis.
d.   take extra care beforehand to ensure that all required data are collected.

Answer: d

21. (obj. 11) Multilevel analysis refers to a procedure in which
   a. students at different grade levels are compared.
   b. the analysis of data is carried out at several levels, such as individual students, classrooms, and schools.
   c. the initial analysis uses simple statistical tests, such as chi-square, and progresses to more sophisticated tests, such as ANOVA.
   d. the appropriate probability level for statistical analysis of a particular data set is determined.

Answer: b

22. (obj. 12) In statistical analyses using a computer, a command file is
   a. the raw data entered into the computer program.
   b. a list of the statistical procedures from which you can choose in analyzing your data.
   c. a summary of the results of the statistical analysis.
   d. a list of the computer instructions that were used to analyze a data set.

Answer: d

OPEN-FORM ITEMS

1. (obj. 1) Why are quantitative researchers more likely than qualitative researchers to use statistics in their investigations?
Answer:
Quantitative researchers collect numerical data, and statistics are needed to analyze the data. Qualitative researchers are less likely to collect numerical data, and therefore they are less likely to use statistics in their data analyses.

2. (obj. 2) A researcher collects data from a sample of school principals on the following variables: (a) age; (b) gender; (c) whether the principal's school is at the elementary, middle, or high school level; and (d) whether the principal was rated as an active or passive learner on a measure of learning styles. Identify the type of score that would be yielded by a measure of each of these variables.
Answer:
   a. Continuous score.
   b. True dichotomy.
   c. Category.
   d. Artificial dichotomy.

3. (obj. 3) If researchers want to know whether boys are more homogeneous in visual-spatial ability than girls, would they use a measure of central tendency, a measure of variability, or a correlational method?
Answer:
A measure of variability.

4. (obj. 4) State one advantage and one disadvantage of the median as a measure of central tendency.
Answer:
An advantage is that the median is not affected by extreme scores. A disadvantage is that the median is less stable than the mean, especially with a small number of cases.

5. (obj. 5) If a sample's scores on a test form a normal curve, what is one piece of information that the standard deviation provides?
Answer (any 1 OK):
   a. The standard deviation tells the percentage of individuals in the sample who earned scores within a given range of standard deviation units.
   b. An individual's standard deviation score indicates his percentile in the distribution of scores for the sample.

6. (obj. 6) What does a test of statistical significance of the difference between the mean scores of two groups tell the researcher about her null hypothesis?
Answer:
If the difference is significant, the null hypothesis is rejected and the researcher concludes that the difference between the sample means probably reflects a true difference between the population means.

7. (obj. 7)
   a. What is statistical power?
   b. Briefly describe two factors that increase statistical power.
Answer:
   a. Statistical power is the probability that a particular test of statistical significance will lead to the rejection of the null hypothesis.
   b. Factors that Increase Statistical Power (any 2 OK):
      (1) Increasing the sample size.
      (2) Raising the level of significance (e.g., from .01 to .05).
      (3) Stating a directional hypothesis.
      (4) Increasing the anticipated effect size (i.e., the magnitude of the difference or of the relationship obtained in the research).

8. (obj. 8) A researcher compares the scores of 1,000 randomly selected 14-year-old urban students with 1,000 randomly selected rural students on a 200-item test of mathematical understanding. The urban sample obtained a mean raw score of 106.54, while the rural sample obtained a mean raw score of 104.55. The standard deviation is 32. The difference between the mean scores is significant at the .05 level. Would you consider this difference to be of practical significance? Why or why not?

Answer:

No. Statistical significance was reached mainly because of the large sample size. The difference amounts to only 2 points on a 200-item test and thus is not of practical significance.

9. (obj. 9) What are two advantages of organizing data into a stem-and-leaf display for exploratory data analysis?

Answer (any 2 OK):

    a.   The researcher can see the shape of the score distribution.

    b.   The display provokes questions about the data by revealing patterns not shown in a conventional listing of scores.

    c.   The display facilitates the detection of outliers.

10. (obj. 10) Several students in a researcher's sample take a test administered at the start of the study but do not take the test administered at the end of the study. Give one reason why this is a problem.

Answer (any 1 OK):

    a.   The missing data make the statistical analysis more complicated.

    b.   The missing data make it more difficult to interpret the statistical results.

11. (obj. 11) A researcher administers a test of musical knowledge to all students in 30 classrooms and then compares the performance of the boys and girls on this test. If the unit of statistical analysis is the classroom, how would the comparison be made?

Answer:

The mean score of boys and the mean score of girls in each of the 30 classrooms would be computed. Then the 30 mean scores for the boys would be compared with the 30 mean scores of the girls.

12. (obj. 12) State one reason why it is desirable to hold on to one's research data for a period of time after a study has been completed.

Answer (any 1 OK):

    a.   The data could be reanalyzed later to yield additional insights.

    b.   If anyone questions the accuracy of the statistical results, they can be checked by reanalyzing the research data.

APPLICATION PROBLEMS

Problem 1
You are interested in the average gain in reading speed that is made by students who take a speed-reading course. A reading test was given to 250 students before and after they took the course. In looking over the scores, you notice that most students gained 100 to 300 words per minute. However, there are about 40 students who made outstanding gains, ranging from 600 to 1,000 words per minute. Would the mean or the median be a more accurate measure of central tendency, and why?
Sample Answer:
The median would be more accurate than the mean, because it would not be affected as much by the 40 extreme scores.

Problem 2
A researcher finds that the mean score of foster-care students on a final exam in a history course is 95.3, and the mean score of other students is 99.7. A t test of this difference yields a p value of .01. What does the p value tell us about the null hypothesis? Also, what generalization does the p value allow us to make?
Sample Answer:
A p value of .01 usually is sufficient to reject the null hypothesis. Therefore, we can generalize beyond this sample and conclude that there would be a real difference in performance on the exam in the total population of foster-care students and other students that this sample represents.

Problem 3
A researcher has completed a study in which an experimental group of 60 college students was formed into pairs and was requested to ask each other questions in preparation for an examination. A control group of 60 students was requested to quiz themselves in preparation for the same examination. Students' scores on the examination formed the dependent variable. What is the appropriate unit of statistical analysis for determining whether the examination performance of the experimental group differed from that of the control group?
Sample Answer:
The researcher should use each pair of students in the experimental group as the unit of analysis, because the learning of each student probably was affected by her partner. The scores of each pair would be averaged to yield a mean score. Because there are 60 experimental group students, there will be 30 mean scores in the statistical analysis. The unit of analysis for the control group should be the individual, because each student engaged in the learning activity independently of the other students. Thus there will be 60 control group scores in the statistical analysis.

TEACHING ACTIVITIES

Activity 1
Have your students read a research article that contains descriptive and inferential statistics. In class, review with the students each statistic that was used and its purpose in the study. Although some students take a statistics course prior to a course in research methods, they may not have learned how statistics actually are used in research. Activity 1 is helpful because it gives students an opportunity to see statistics in a relevant research context.

Activity 2
Have your students read a research article. In class, discuss with them how the study might be replicated by using the approach of literal replication, operational replication, or constructive replication. The article used for Activity 1 might be used for this purpose as well.

Activity 3
Have each of your students collect data about two variables and bring the data to class. (A simple alternative to this procedure is to ask each student in class to write down the heights of their father and mother or of two acquaintances, one male and one female.) You can list the data for these two variables on the blackboard and show students how you can compute various descriptive statistics about them (e.g., mean, median, mode, range, standard deviation, and effect size). You also can generate a null hypothesis (e.g., there is no significant difference between the height of males and females), and show students how this hypothesis can be accepted or rejected by a t test.

Activity 4
Invite to class a researcher who used computer software in carrying out statistical analyses for a recent study. Ask the researcher to explain how the data were entered into the computer file, how the statistical analyses were done, the kinds of computer printouts that were generated, how to interpret the results, and any problems that arose in the use of the computer.

CHAPTER 6
SELECTING A SAMPLE

Note: The phrase in parentheses following the item number for both closed-form and open-form items, for example, 1. (obj. 3), refers to the textbook chapter objective to which the item is keyed.

CLOSED-FORM ITEMS

1. (obj. 1) Unlike quantitative researchers, qualitative researchers select their samples to
    a. satisfy the requirements of grounded theory.
    b. test theories about the phenomenon being studied.
    c. accurately represent a defined population.
    d. study cases that are information-rich with respect to their research questions.
Answer: d

2. (obj. 1) The most important requirement for being able to generalize the results of a quantitative research study is to
    a. minimize sample attrition and missing data.
    b. formulate a theory and use it to interpret the study's findings.
    c. define a population in advance of data collection and sample from it.
    d. use measures for which population norms are available.
Answer: c

3. (obj. 2) For a study to have population validity,
    a. the study must employ an experimental research design.
    b. the sample must be randomly selected from the defined population.
    c. the study must be a replication of a previous study involving the same population.
    d. subjects must be randomly assigned to the experimental and control groups.
Answer: b

4. (obj. 2) A researcher plans a study in a school district to compare method A and method B of teaching reading. Which of the following approaches would be most likely to ensure a representative sample?
   a. Obtain permission from a cooperative principal to nominate students in his school to experience each teaching method.
   b. Require all students enrolled in English literature classes to serve as subjects.
   c. Use students from one school as subjects to receive method A and students from a comparable school to receive the method B.
   d. Define the population as all students in the district receiving reading instruction, select a random sample, and randomly assign students to methods A or B.

Answer: d

5. (obj. 2) Replication logic refers to
   a. the conduct of replications of a study with samples from different populations to determine the stability of the findings.
   b. the use of theory to determine the other types of cases to which the findings of one case study can be generalized.
   c. the cross-validation of research hypotheses through repeated replications of the original study.
   d. the precise specification of a population so that subsequent researchers can draw equivalent samples in an effort to replicate the original study's findings.

Answer: b

6. (obj. 2) If a qualitative researcher is doing a theoretical replication, the next case to be studied should
   a. differ from the first case in ways that allow a further test of the theory.
   b. be similar to the first case.
   c. yield similar results to the findings obtained from the first case.
   d. be selected to test alternate interpretations of the findings from the first case.

Answer: a

7. (obj. 3) All the members of a set of persons to whom a researcher wishes to generalize the results of a study are referred to as
   a. the defined population.
   b. the accessible population.
   c. the target population.
   d. the sampling distribution.

Answer: c

8. (obj. 3) Another term corresponding to *target population* in quantitative research is
   a. accessible population.
   b. universe.
   c. defined population.
   d. cohort.
Answer: b

9. (obj. 4) Population validity is achieved only if
   a. the researcher limits generalizations of the study's findings to the accessible population.
   b. a test effectively predicts a relevant variable within the target population.
   c. the accessible population is randomly selected from the target population.
   d. the accessible population is reasonably representative of the target population.
Answer: d

10. (obj. 4) Which of the following is an important criterion for determining whether an experiment has population validity?
   a. A clear description of the target population.
   b. A detailed description of the sampling procedure.
   c. Identification and description of the sampling frame.
   d. all of the above.
Answer: d

11. (obj. 5) Picking names out of a hat is an example of
   a. simple random sampling.
   b. systematic sampling.
   c. cluster sampling.
   d. sampling error.
Answer: a

12. (obj. 5) An investigator wants to compare the reading comprehension of first-grade students who are taught reading by the whole-language method (treatment A) versus the phonetic method (treatment B). He selects all first graders in Washington Elementary School (6 classes, $N = 200$) and places their names in a hat. The first 60 names taken from the hat are placed in treatment A, and the next 60 names are placed in treatment B. What procedure has the researcher used?
   a. Simple random sampling.
   b. Random assignment.
   c. Cluster sampling.
   d. Stratified sampling.
Answer: b

13. (obj. 5) Stratified sampling usually is a better approach than random sampling if the researcher
   a. wants to avoid sampling bias.
   b. is studying a target population that is highly homogeneous.
   c. expects small differences between the groups being compared.
   d. wants to study the performance of different subgroups within the sample.
Answer: d

14. (obj. 5) In doing a survey of Chicago residents' evaluation of their schools, the researcher divides the city into 9-square-block areas and randomly selects 20 areas for study. This is an example of
   a. stratified sampling.
   b. cluster sampling.
   c. subgroup analysis.
   d. use of a large sample.
Answer: b

15. (obj. 5) A disadvantage of cluster sampling compared to other sampling techniques is that
   a. one cannot use conventional formulas for computing statistics on the data.
   b. it requires including subjects in the sample from every sampling unit.
   c. this technique is more expensive than other sampling techniques.
   d. it rejects randomization as a basis for sample selection.
Answer: a

16. (obj. 6) The problem of attrition (loss of subjects) is best reduced by
   a. using systematic sampling techniques.
   b. using volunteers as subjects.
   c. fostering subjects' commitment to the study and maintaining rapport with subjects.
   d. including subgroups of subjects proportional to their numbers in the population.
Answer: c

17. (obj. 6) Put an L before the following research situations that require a large sample and an S before those situations in which a small sample is acceptable.
   __ a.   Many uncontrolled variables are present.
   __ b.   Large relationships are anticipated between the variables to be correlated.
   __ c.   Subgroup analyses are to be performed.
   __ d.   The subjects have been closely matched on the critical variables.
   __ e.   Small differences are expected between the experimental and control groups' scores on the dependent variable.
Answer: a=L, b=S, c=L, d=S, e=L

18. (obj. 6) A small sample is most appropriate when
   a. small differences are anticipated between the experimental and control groups.
   b. subgroup analyses are planned.
   c. the population is highly heterogeneous on the variables being studied.
   d. close matching of the comparison groups is possible.
Answer: d

19. (obj. 6) The first step in estimating needed sample size is to
   a. determine the size of the target population.
   b. determine the size of the accessible population.
   c. study the findings of related research using similar variables.
   d. determine the population mean and standard deviation for each variable of concern.
Answer: c

20. (obj. 7) Sampling techniques are more flexible in qualitative research than in quantitative research mainly because qualitative researchers
   a. need only one or a few cases.
   b. are interested in typical cases.
   c. prefer emergent research designs.
   d. have no interest in generalizing study results.
Answer: c

21. (obj. 8) In a study of teachers' use of power, selecting as a case a teacher who is known throughout the state as an exceptionally active opinion maker would be an example of
    a. typical case sampling.
    b. intensity sampling.
    c. deviant case sampling.
    d. convenience sampling.
Answer: c

22. (obj. 8) Random sampling in qualitative research sometimes is used in order to
    a. ensure that the cases studied are representative.
    b. establish that the sampling procedure is not biased.
    c. confirm the findings of previous case studies.
    d. select cases that illustrate the full range of variation in the phenomena studied.
Answer: b

23. (obj. 9) A qualitative researcher who is interested in the study of a phenomenon in depth would be well advised to
    a. study a wide range of experiences for a small number of people.
    b. study a narrow set of experiences for a large number of people.
    c. document the naturally occurring diversity and variation of a phenomenon.
    d. use stratified purposeful sampling to select the cases.
Answer: a

24. (obj. 10) Volunteers are likely to constitute a biased sample because they
    a. have been found to differ from nonvolunteers on numerous characteristics.
    b. are less responsive to experimental interventions than subjects who are required to participate.
    c. they more susceptible to the Hawthorne effect than nonvolunteers.
    d. they tend to have more conservative attitudes than nonvolunteers.
Answer: a

25. (obj. 10) Compared to nonvolunteers, volunteers tend to be
    a. more introverted.
    b. lower in need for achievement.
    c. better educated.
    d. more conforming.
Answer: c

26. (obj. 10) If it is necessary to use volunteers in a research study, the researcher should
   a. consider whether volunteers are likely to differ from nonvolunteers on critical variables.
   b. increase the sample size.
   c. require a public commitment to participate.
   d. keep the description of the study's purpose brief and matter-of-fact.

Answer: a

27. (obj. 11) Which of the following is an effective method for recruiting individuals to participate in a research study?
   a. Make the study sound appealing.
   b. Offer gifts and other benefits to prospective participants.
   c. Have the request for volunteers made by a person of high status.
   d. all of the above.

Answer: d

OPEN-FORM ITEMS

1. (obj. 1) A researcher randomly selects a sample of 100 teachers from inner-city schools in a large U.S. city. She views her sample as representative of the defined population of all inner-city school teachers in the United States. The researcher measures the teachers' attitudes toward site-based management of schools. If her study has population validity, what can she conclude from the results of the study?

Answer: The researcher can conclude that the results she obtained for this sample of inner-city school teachers would be similar if she had measured the attitudes of the entire population of inner-city school teachers in the U.S., that is, she can generalize her findings from the sample to the defined population.

2. (obj. 1) A qualitative researcher who is interested in studying school teachers who moonlight in other jobs decides to select cases who have only one extra job, at which they spend no more than 10 hours a week.

    a.   What type of purposeful sample does the researcher appear to be seeking?

    b.   What is the researcher's probable rationale for limiting the study to such cases?

Answer:

    a.   This appears to be an typical-case sample, in which the researcher wishes to study cases who represent the majority of moonlighting teachers rather than intense or extreme cases who moonlight far less or far more than 10 hours a week.

    b.   By studying less extreme cases the researcher is more likely to obtain findings that will deepen the understanding of the general effects of moonlighting on teachers and their students.

3. (obj. 2) How does an educational researcher establish the population validity of his research study?

Answer: Population validity is established by demonstrating that the sample is representative of the target population to which the researcher wishes to generalize his findings. It can be established by showing that the sample was randomly selected from the accessible population and that the accessible population in turn represents the target population.

4. (obj. 2) Describe one type of replication that a qualitative researcher might carry out.

Answer (any 1 OK):

    a.   The researcher can do a literal replication, in which she selects a case for whom she predicts similar results to those for the case or cases previously studied.

    b.   The researcher can do a theoretical replication, in which she selects a case for whom she predicts the results will differ from those for the case or cases previously studied in ways consistent with the theory underlying the research.

5. (obj. 3) What is the difference between a target population and an accessible population?

Answer: The target population is the population to which you want to generalize your results, and the accessible population is the population from which you draw your sample.

6. (obj. 3) Define *sampling* as this term is used in quantitative research.

Answer: In quantitative research, sampling is the process of selecting a sample from a defined population so that the sample accurately represents the population.

7. (obj. 4) Describe one criterion that should be satisfied in order to determine that a research study has high population validity.
Answer (any 1 OK):

    a.   The researcher should provide a clear description of the target population to which she intends to generalize the results.

    b.   The researcher should describe the sampling procedure to be used, including type of sampling technique, sample size, and geographic area in which the accessible population is located.

    c.   The researcher should describe the sampling frame, that is, the list or source from which the sample was selected.

    d.   The researcher should include information about the completion rate, that is, the proportion of the original sample for whom complete data were obtained.

8. (obj. 5) Explain the difference between random sampling and random assignment in experimental research.
Answer: Random sampling means that every individual in the accessible population has an equal chance of being selected for the sample. Random assignment involves the use of randomization procedures to ensure that each individual in the sample has an equal chance of being in the experimental or control group.

9. (obj. 5) State one reason why, if all other things are equal, randomly selected samples are preferable for research purposes in quantitative research.
Answer (any 1 OK):

    a.   Random samples yield research data that can be generalized to a larger population within margins of error that can be estimated by statistical techniques.

    b.   Random sampling satisfies the logic by which a null hypothesis is tested with inferential statistics.

10. (obj. 5) Name one condition under which it would be appropriate to use nonproportional stratified sampling, that is, to select an equal number of subjects from each stratum rather than selecting from each stratum the same proportion that exists in the target population.
Answer (any 1 OK):

    a.   You are concerned primarily with the performance of subjects in each of the strata rather than with comparing the performance of subjects in different strata.

    b.   You want to be sure you have enough cases in each of the strata for your analysis.

    c.   You do not intend to compute means or other statistics for the entire sample.

11. (obj. 5) You wish to obtain a simple random sample of 1,000 members of the American Psychological Association to whom you will send a questionnaire about their views concerning the appropriate preparation of clinical psychologists. List the steps you would take in selecting your sample.

Answer:
  a. Obtain a list of members and number the names on the list.
  b. Using a table of random numbers to at least four digits, select 1,000 numbers.
  c. Identify those 1,000 members on the member list who have the selected numbers.

12. (obj. 5) Suppose that you are planning a study on the relationship between teachers' use of six verbal behaviors (specific praise, prompting, etc.) and student achievement. Your accessible population includes all fourth-, fifth-, and sixth-grade teachers in the Chicago public schools, who previously have been classified as either bilingual or English-speaking-only. Your sample will include a total of 120 teachers.

  a. What sampling procedure should you use to ensure that you have an adequate sample of teachers at each grade level, including both bilingual and English-speaking-only teachers?

  b. How would you carry out the sampling procedure?

Answer:
  a. You should use stratified sampling.
  b. Divide the accessible population into six groups: fourth-grade bilingual, fourth grade English-speaking-only, fifth-grade bilingual, fifth-grade English-speaking-only, sixth-grade bilingual, and sixth-grade English-speaking-only. Then randomly select 20 teachers from each group.

13. (obj. 6) Briefly describe three types of research situations that require a fairly large sample size.

Answer (any 3 OK):
  a. Many uncontrolled variables are present.
  b. Small changes or small differences between the comparison groups are expected on the dependent variables.
  c. The research design calls for breaking the sample into subgroups.
  d. The population is highly heterogeneous on the variables being studied.
  e. Reliable measures are not available.
  f. High attrition is expected.
  g. A high level of statistical significance or statistical power is required.

14. (obj. 7) When using purposeful sampling, what does the researcher strive to accomplish in selecting the sample?
Answer: The selection of cases that are likely to be information-rich in relation to the specific phenomena being studied.

15. (obj. 7) Describe one rationale that a qualitative researcher can use to justify her selection of a particular case to study.
Answer (any 1 OK):
    a.   The particular case will enable her to develop a deeper understanding of the phenomenon being studied.
    b. The particular case will enable her to discover or test theories about the phenomenon.
    c. The particular case will enable her to generalize the findings to other, similar cases.

16. (obj. 8) Briefly name and describe *three* purposeful sampling strategies.
Answer:
(Note: See pages 231-235 in the textbook, which describes 14 purposeful sampling strategies and a 15th strategy, opportunistic sampling. Any 3 of these 15 strategies is OK.)

17. (obj. 9) Give one reason why a qualitative researcher might find it desirable to study more than one case in a research study.
Answer (any 1 OK):
    a.   The researcher wishes to document the diversity or variations in a phenomenon that are reflected in different individuals' experience.
    b.   The researcher wishes to conduct a literal replication to increase the certainty of the findings for one case.
    c.   The researcher wishes to conduct a theoretical replication in order to determine if the results for the next case are different from those for the previous case in a theoretically consistent way.

18. (obj. 10) List three characteristics that researchers have found to differ for volunteer and non-volunteer subjects.
Answer:
(Note: See figure 6.1 in the textbook, which lists 11 characteristics of research volunteers; any 3 of these characteristics are OK.)

19. (obj. 11) State three suggestions for increasing the proportion of volunteers and thus reducing volunteer bias.

Answer:

(Note: See figure 6.2 in the textbook, which lists 11 suggestions for improving the rate of volunteering to participate in a research study; any 3 of these suggestions are OK.)

APPLICATION PROBLEMS

Problem 1

1. A researcher wants to do a case study of the emotional reactions and motivational states of a child while playing computer games.

    a. What rationale can he use to justify generalizing about the results of the case study?

    b. How could he increase the generalizability of his case study findings?

Sample Answer:

    a. If the researcher describes the student's characteristics to demonstrate that the student is typical of a larger group of students, he is justified in generalizing the findings to that larger group.

    b. The researcher can increase the generalizability of his findings by using literal or theoretical replication and doing multiple case studies.

Problem 2

An investigator wishes to study the oral reading performance of second-grade students in a large school district. A total of 3,172 second-grade students are enrolled in 104 classrooms in the district. The investigator wishes to obtain a total group of 100 subjects using a two-stage cluster sampling technique. Describe the steps she would take in selecting her sample.

Sample Answer:

    a. Identify the 104 second-grade classrooms and assign each classroom a number.

    b. Randomly select 10 classrooms using a table of random numbers, or by drawing numbers from a container.

    c. Obtain the names of all students in the selected classrooms, and assign each student a number.

    d. Randomly select 10 students from each of the 10 classrooms using a table of random numbers.

Problem 3

A researcher is studying the effects of learning a problem-solving strategy upon the mathematics achievement of sixth-grade students. He selects a sample of students in one school and randomly assigns half of them to the experimental group and half to the control group. All students will be given a pretest of mathematics achievement. The experimental group then will receive a one-hour lesson that teaches a problem-solving strategy for students to use in solving word problems in mathematics. The control group receives conventional instruction. Because he expects the problem-solving training to work best with the brighter students, the researcher divides both groups into two subgroups based on their IQ scores, using the following categories: below 90, 90-110, 111-130, and above 130. He administers a mathematics achievement posttest to all subjects two months after the treatment ends. Explain why a fairly large sample size is required for this project.

Sample Answer:

a.   Because the treatment lasts only one hour and involves only word problems, the researcher might well expect only a small difference in the groups' posttest mathematics achievement.

b.   In an average school population, only a very small percentage of the students are likely to have IQ scores above 130. Because the researcher has broken his sample into subgroups based on IQ level, he must obtain a large enough sample to ensure that he has enough subjects in this category.

Problem 4

Identify the procedures in the following research description that are likely to cause sampling bias: A researcher teaches three sections of a Remedial English class for freshmen in a large state university. A colleague teaches three sections of regular Freshman English. The researcher has developed a special 20-hour program to teach rules of spelling. She gives a spelling test in her sections and in her colleague's sections. She identifies 63 students from her sections and 36 from her colleague's sections who scored below 50 percent on the test. She then describes the special program to her sections and asks the 63 low scorers to take the program by attending special sessions one hour per day for four weeks. Fifty-one agree to do so. The 36 students in her colleague's sections are used as a control group and receive no special treatment. At the end of four weeks, 26 of her students have completed the spelling program, while the remainder have missed between 1 and 18 of the sessions. She administers a spelling posttest to the 26 treatment subjects and the 36 control subjects and compares their gains since the pretest.

Sample Answer:

a. The subjects were a sample of convenience, rather than being drawn systematically from a defined population.

b. The treatment group consisted entirely of volunteers.

c. The treatment group suffered a large loss of subjects, and the subjects who completed the program probably were highly motivated by comparison. No control-group subjects were lost, because they were not required to do anything.

d. Subjects were not drawn from the same subject pool. That is, the experimental group was drawn from the remedial course, whereas the control group was drawn from the regular course. Because subjects were drawn from different populations, they probably differed in ways that affected the study results, e.g., their overall mastery of English.

Problem 5

Describe a qualitative research problem for which intensity sampling would be a good purposeful sampling strategy.

Sample Answer:

a.   The researcher wishes to do an indepth study in which he asks a small number of students to reflect freely on their feelings and thoughts related to a specific phenomenon, e.g., their experiences with loneliness in school or their jealousy about another student's success. The researcher would not seek extreme manifestations of the phenomena of interest because they might not lend themselves to the reflective process, but would seek intense manifestations of the phenomena so that there is enough to study.

b.   In evaluating an instructional program that has been implemented in many schools, the researcher might want to avoid selecting either extreme successes or unusual failures, that might be discredited as being too extreme or unusual for providing trustworthy information. Therefore, the evaluator would select cases that manifest sufficient success or failure to illuminate the nature of the phenomenon but do not fall at the extreme.

TEACHING ACTIVITIES

Activity 1

Ask students to identify a quantitative research problem they are studying or might want to study. Ask each student to describe a relevant target population to whom they wish to generalize the results of their study, an accessible population from which they could draw a sample, and the sampling technique described in the textbook that appears most appropriate for selecting the sample.

Activity 2

Have students identify an educational phenomenon on which they would like to shed light by doing a case study. Have them describe some of the characteristics they would look for in the case selected for study if they were to use (a) extreme or deviant case sampling, (b) intensity sampling, or (c) typical case sampling.

Activity 3

Have all students read the same qualitative case study. During class time, have students (a) identify the purposeful sampling strategy that was used, (b) discuss what this strategy enabled the researcher to learn about the phenomena of interest, and (c) whether another sampling strategy might have been more appropriate.

CHAPTER 7
COLLECTING RESEARCH DATA WITH TESTS AND SELF-REPORT MEASURES

Note: The phrase in parentheses following the item number for both closed-form and open-form items, for example, 1. (obj. 3), refers to the textbook chapter objective to which the item is keyed.

CLOSED-FORM ITEMS

1. (obj. 1) The objectivity of a standardized test refers to its
   a. degree of relationship to a criterion variable.
   b. freedom from tester bias.
   c. accuracy of prediction.
   d. provision of normative data.
Answer: b

2. (obj. 1) To standardize a test, the developer must establish
   a. the test's validity.
   b. the test's reliability.
   c. procedures that ensure consistency in how the test is administered and scored.
   d. all of the above.
Answer: c

3. (obj. 2) Match each example of evidence about a test below with the type of validity that it represents.
   __ 1. The test was found to include 32 of the 47 topics covered in a textbook.
   __ 2. The test was found to lead to a higher rate of referral for boys than for girls to a treatment program for attention deficit disorder.
   __ 3. Students' rank order of performance on the test was found to correspond well to the students' rank order of performance on an established longer test of the same ability.
   __ 4. The test was found to be a good measure of students' ability to learn independently.
   a. Concurrent validity.
   b. Consequential validity.
   c. Construct validity.
   d. Content validity.
Answer: 1=d, 2=b, 3=a, 4=c

4. (obj. 2) Test validity is
    a. not a unitary concept.
    b. an intrinsic property of the test.
    c. an intrinsic property of the test scores.
    d. a property of the inferences that are made from test scores.
Answer: d

5. (obj. 3) Match each example of test reliability below with the type of reliability
coefficient that is used to calculate it.
    __ 1. After the test is administered, it is split into two halves and the scores on
           one half are correlated with those on the other half.
    __ 2. Two parallel forms of the test are administered, and scores on one form are
           correlated with those on the other form.
    __ 3. The test is administered and then readministered after a time delay, and
           scores from the first administration are correlated with those from the
           second administration.
    __ 4. Individual test items are analyzed by using standard formulas.
    a. Coefficient of equivalence.
    b. Coefficient alpha.
    c. Coefficient of internal consistency.
    d. Coefficient of stability.
Answer: 1=c, 2=a, 3=d, 4=b

6. (obj. 3) A test is reliable to the extent that it
    a. yields scores that are interpreted the same way by different raters.
    b. measures a known construct.
    c. contains nonrandom measurement error.
    d. minimizes measurement error.
Answer: d

7. (obj. 4) The various types of measurement error in a test can be estimated by
    a. classical test theory.
    b. generalizability theory.
    c. the standard error of measurement.
    d. coefficient alpha.
Answer: b

8. (obj. 5) When the researcher has the choice of using a standardized test or an achievement test constructed by the teachers who are being studied, the researcher
   a. should use the teacher-constructed test, because such tests generally are freer of measurement error.
   b. should use the teacher-constructed test, because such tests generally have better concurrent validity.
   c. should use the standardized test, because such tests generally are better written.
   d. can use either test, because both types of test have similar strengths and weaknesses.

Answer: c

9. (obj. 6) The interpretation of an individual's test score by comparing it to the scores earned by other individuals is referred to as
   a. norm-referenced measurement.
   b. individual-referenced measurement.
   c. domain-referenced measurement.
   d. objectives-referenced measurement.

Answer: a

10. (obj. 6) A prespecified standard of performance is most important in
   a. norm-referenced measurement.
   b. individual-referenced measurement.
   c. criterion-referenced measurement.
   d. objectives-referenced measurement.

Answer: c

11. (obj. 7) It usually is better to administer an individual test than a group test when
   a. it is necessary to ensure standard conditions of administration.
   b. a high degree of objectivity in scoring is desired.
   c. it is necessary to obtain data on all research participants within a short period of time.
   d. the researcher is interested in the process by which the overall score is obtained.

Answer: d

12. (obj. 8) Match each of the following types of test with the appropriate definition.
    __ 1.   Intelligence tests.
    __ 2.   Aptitude tests.
    __ 3.   Achievement test batteries.
    __ 4.   Diagnostic tests.
    a.   Estimate general intellectual level by sampling performance on various tasks.
    b.   Aim at predicting performance on future tasks.
    c.   Provide scores indicating individuals' strengths and weaknesses in a given area of the curriculum.
    d.   Measure knowledge or mastery of a variety of content areas.
Answer: 1=a, 2=b, 3=d, 4=c

13. (obj. 9) Which of the following is *not* an appropriate criterion for judging the validity of inferences drawn from a performance assessment?
    a.   whether all students had an equal opportunity to acquire the expertise measured by the test.
    b.   the extent to which the test scores correlate with the test-takers' scores on a well-established standardized test.
    c.   the extent to which the test's content represents the content domain covered during instruction.
    d.   the cost of administering the test.
Answer: b

14. (obj. 9) The hermeneutic approach to test reliability
    a.   requires test scorers to reach a consensus about the score or rating that each test-taker will receive.
    b.   requires administration of parallel forms of a test.
    c.   involves identifying experts with a consistent perspective to score the tests.
    d.   involves the calculation of a standard error of measurement.
Answer: a

15. (obj. 10) To determine an individual's unique structuring of reality, the researcher is advised to administer a
    a.   variety of attitude scales.
    b.   personality inventory.
    c.   combination of attitude scales and a personality inventory.
    d.   projective test.
Answer: d

94

16. (obj. 11) The *Mental Measurement Yearbooks* are particularly helpful for
    a. determining the latest trends in assessment methodology.
    b. identifying procedures that can be used to establish a test's validity and reliability.
    c. obtaining a list of tests that are available for measuring a particular variable.
    d. obtaining a statistical summary of the test scores of students with different demographic characteristics.

Answer c

17. (obj. 12) Contacting the test developer directly is particularly useful when you wish to obtain
    a. tables of norms for the test.
    b. recent information about the test that has not been published.
    c. reliability and validity information about the test.
    d. information about how to administer and score the test.

Answer: b

18. (obj. 13) In computer-adaptive testing, the test-taker
    a. responds only to items that are at a moderate level of difficulty.
    b. is allowed as much time as he wishes to respond to each item.
    c. responds to items that are matched to his ability level.
    d. is allowed to choose the items to which he will respond.

Answer: c

19. (obj. 14) The process by which items are placed on a scale in order of relative difficulty in computer-adaptive testing is based on
    a. item response theory.
    b. generalizability theory.
    c. classical test theory.
    d. individual-referenced measurement.

Answer: a

20. (obj. 15) In test development, the purpose of item analysis is to determine
    a. the difficulty level of each test item.
    b. the reliability of each test item.
    c. the validity of each test item.
    d. all of the above.

Answer: d

21. (obj. 15) Put the following steps of test development in the order that they usually occur.
   a. Developing a prototype.
   b. Defining the constructs to be measured.
   c. Reviewing related tests that have been developed.
   d. Collecting data on the test's validity and reliability.

Answer: b, c, a, d

22. (obj. 16) Which of the following actions by the researcher is least likely to be helpful if protestors question the administration of a certain test in a research study?
   a. Defending the test by reviewing with the protestors the merits of each item on the test.
   b. Demonstrating how the test as a whole is valid and reliable.
   c. Demonstrating that the test follows the guidelines in the *Standards for Educational and Psychological Testing.*
   d. Offering to withdraw individuals from the study if they do not wish to take the test.

Answer: a

23. (obj. 17) Match each testing procedure below with the outcome for which it is intended.
   __ 1. Have the teacher tell the students (the research participants) that the test is important and that they should try to do their best.
   __ 2. Remind the research participants that data collected on any particular individual will not be revealed.
   __ 3. Emphasize the official nature of the testing session.
   a. You want to ensure that the research participants depict themselves in a typical, honest manner.
   b. You want to obtain the research participants' maximal performance.
   c. You want to enhance the research participants' cooperation.

Answer: 1=b, 2=a, 3=c

OPEN-FORM ITEMS

1. (obj. 1) Describe three criteria for judging the quality of a test.
Answer (any 3 OK):

    a.   Objectivity, that is, the extent to which the test's scores are free from bias by the individuals who administer and score it.

    b.   Standard conditions for administering and scoring the test.

    c.   Whether the test scores can be interpreted by using a set of norms derived from a large sample representing a defined population.

    d. The extent to which inferences from the test's scores are valid, that is, appropriate, meaningful, and useful.

    e.   The extent to which the test scores are reliable, that is, free of measurement error.

2. (obj. 2) A researcher uses a theory of academic self-esteem to identify five behavior patterns that are indicative of level of students' level of academic self-esteem, such as the frequency of positive statements students make about themselves. The researcher next observes 50 students for one month and records the frequency of these behavior patterns for each student. Finally, the researcher develops a paper-and-pencil test of academic self-esteem and correlates the students' scores with their level of academic self-esteem based on the observations. What type of test validity has the researcher established?
Answer:
Construct validity.

3. (obj. 3) A researcher has developed a new test designed to measure musical aptitude. She selects a random sample of 200 college freshmen and administers the test to them. One month later she again administers the test to the same students and computes a correlation coefficient between the two sets of scores. What type of reliability does this coefficient indicate?
Answer (any 1 OK):

    a.   Test-retest reliability.

    b.   Coefficient of stability.

4. (obj. 4) An investigator administers a reading achievement test that has a mean of 220, a standard deviation of 20, and a standard error of measurement of 5. Mary obtains a score of 235. Using the standard error of measurement (sm), what estimate can we make of her true score?

Answer (any 1 OK):

   a. There are about two chances in three that Mary's true score is 235 $\pm$ 1 sm, that is, between 230 and 240.

   b. There is a 95 percent chance that her true score is 235 $\pm$ 2 sm, that is, between 225 and 245.

5. (obj. 5) The superintendent tells a researcher who is conducting a study in her district that he should use achievement tests constructed by the teachers to measure student learning rather than a standardized achievement test. How can the researcher defend the decision to use a standardized test?

Answer:

The researcher can note that teacher-constructed tests are useful for certain purposes but not for research. Research requires tests that have standard conditions of administration and scoring, as well as tables of norms. Only standardized tests satisfy these requirements.

6. (obj. 6) A student earns a score of 85 on a 100-item achievement test. How would this score be interpreted if the test was criterion-referenced?

Answer:

The score would be compared to a prespecified standard of performance. For example, if the standard is a score of 90, we would conclude that the student did not achieve the criterion level of performance.

7. (obj. 7) Describe one situation in which an individually administered test would be preferable to a group-administered test.

Answer (any 1 OK):

   a. When the researcher wishes to study the process by which an individual arrives at an answer or response to a test item.

   b. When the individuals to be tested have a limited attention span or other condition that would impair their performance if tested in a group situation.

   c. When the individuals to be tested cannot read the test directions and items.

8. (obj. 8) Give one reason why the test ceiling is an important factor to consider in selecting an achievement test to use in a research study.

Answer (any 1 OK):

    a.   If the test is too easy, it will not reflect how much students know.

    b.   If the test is too easy, it will not reflect how their learning has improved as a result of an experimental intervention.

9. (obj. 9) Some school districts require candidates for a teaching position to teach an actual lesson, which is rated for quality. The district also may require candidates to submit a collection of curriculum materials and lesson plans that they have prepared in their previous teaching positions.

    a.   What is this approach to measurement called?

    b.   What is the technical name for the collection of completed work?

Answer:

    a.   This approach is called *performance assessment*.

    b.   The technical name is *portfolio*.

10. (obj. 10) Describe at least one advantage and one disadvantage of self-report personality measures.

Answer:

    Advantages

    a.   These measures are inexpensive and easy to administer.

    b.   They often can be scored by machine.

    c.   Norms often are available for these measures.

    Disadvantages

    a.   These measures are based on self-report and thus a respondent can lie or mislead the investigator if he wants to. Also, the responses are subject to distortion due to inaccurate self-perceptions.

    b.   They can be attacked as an invasion of privacy.

    c.   They are subject to faking.

    d.   They are subject to response sets.

11. (obj. 11) What is the purpose of the *Mental Measurement Yearbooks*?

Answer:

The *Mental Measurement Yearbooks* provide a comprehensive list of tests, information about each test, and a critique of many of them.

12. (obj. 12) State one reason why it is important for a researcher to examine an actual copy of an achievement test before deciding to use it in a study.
Answer (any 1 OK):

    a.   To decide whether the test is content valid for the situation in which the researcher plans to use it.

    b.   To determine whether the test's reading level for the research sample is appropriate.

    c.   To determine whether there might be problems in administering or scoring the test.

13. (obj. 13) State two advantages of administering a test in computer format.
Answer (any 2 OK):

    a.   The order in which the test items are presented can be varied for each individual who takes the test.

    b.   The amount of time that each item is exposed to the test taker can be controlled.

    c.   The opportunity for test-takers to look back or ahead to other sections of the test can be controlled.

    d.   Scoring of the test is easier and more accurate.

    e.   The test can be administered by using the principles of item response theory.

14. (obj. 14)
What is one advantage of using item response theory to develop an achievement test?
Answer (any 1 OK):

    a.   Test administration is more efficient.

    b.   Test takers are not frustrated by test items that are too difficult or easy for them.

    c.   The testing time necessary to obtain valid estimates of test-takers' ability is shorter.

15. (obj. 15) Describe one procedure that customarily is used as part of an item analysis of a test under development.
Answer (any 1 OK):

    a.   An item validity coefficient is computed to determine how well individuals' scores on each item correlate with their scores on a criterion measure.

    b.   An item reliability coefficient is computed to determine how well individuals' scores on each item correlate with their total test scores.

    c.   If it is a performance test, a difficulty index is computed to determine the percentage of individuals who answer each item correctly.

16. (obj. 16) How can the publication *Standards for Educational and Psychological Testing* help if a test to be administered as part of a research study comes under attack?
Answer:
The researcher can use it to demonstrate that professional standards for testing exist and that her test and procedures for administering it meet those standards.

17. (obj. 17) A researcher plans to administer a personality measure and wants to ensure that the research sample gives honest responses to its items. What is one procedure that the researcher can use to accomplish this goal?
Answer (any 1 OK):
    a. Assure the subjects that their responses will be kept confidential.
    b. Have individuals write a code number on the measure rather than their names.
    c. Inform the subjects that the research results will be presented in group form only.

APPLICATION PROBLEMS

Problem 1
An investigator has developed a new technique to teach eighth-grade students the characteristics of positive and negative numbers. She wishes to evaluate the technique by using it to teach group A. Group B, which receives conventional instruction on positive and negative numbers, serves as a control. She needs a mathematics achievement test to measure the posttraining performance of the two groups. She considers the XYZ Test of Mathematics Achievement. In checking the test manual, she finds that when this test was administered to a sample of eighth-grade students at the end of the academic year, the test scores correlated .72 with their end-of-year grades in mathematics. No other validity evidence was given in the test manual.
    a. What type of validity evidence was given in the test manual?
    b. What type of validity is most relevant to the proposed study, and why?
Sample Answer:
    a. Evidence of concurrent validity was given, because the test scores and grades both measure the same construct and were obtained at the same time.
    b. Content validity is most relevant, because the training was concerned with a limited content area. Most regular achievement tests would be inappropriate because they deal mainly with content not covered in the new instructional technique. What is needed is a measure that deals only with positive and negative numbers. This can be determined only by comparing the test content with the training content.

Problem 2

Describe a procedure for handling each of these testing problems.

    a.   A researcher is planning to administer several aptitude tests to groups of college students as part of a research project. What can he do to increase the likelihood that students will give their maximum performance?

    b.   A researcher wants to administer a measure of sexual attitudes to high school and college students. What can she do to increase the likelihood that students will give frank, honest responses?

Sample Answer:

    a.   Make the testing appear to be important. Tell the students you will tell them the purpose of the research after the testing is completed.

    b.   Before administering the measure, tell students that the individuals' responses will not be revealed to anyone and that results will be reported in group form only. It also is desirable not to oblige subjects to write their names on the measure; if later identification is needed, code numbers can be used.

Problem 3
(Note to the instructor: You may wish to update this application problem using a more recent edition of the *Mental Measurements Yearbook*.)
Locate tests in the *Ninth Mental Measurements Yearbook* that measure study skills. You are planning research to investigate the relationship between study skills and school achievement. You plan to test a random sample of students at grades 4 through 12.

    a.   Which index(es) in the *Yearbook* would you check to locate measures of study skills?

    b.   List the tests and test numbers you locate that measure study skills. Place an asterisk in front of those that provide a study skills score for the entire grade range of your study (i.e., 4-12).

    c.   Why would the Bristol Achievement Tests: Study Skills (171) probably not be appropriate for your research project?

<u>Sample Answer:</u>

    a.   The Score Index should be used. Nine test numbers are listed.

    b.   Tests measuring study skills:

Test Number	Test Name
24	Achievement Tests: Grades 1-8
*123	Basic Skills Inventory
168	Bristol Achievement Tests (the Study Skills subtest is the same as 171)
171	Bristol Achievement Tests: Study Skills
660	Mastery: An Evaluation Tool
*670	McCarthy Individualized Diagnostic Reading Inventory, Revised Edition
699	Metropolitan Achievement Test, 5th Edition
*1115	Sequential Tests of Educational Progress, Series III
*1293	The 3-R's Test

    c.   The Bristol Achievement Tests were developed and standardized in England and Wales. Therefore, the test content might not be appropriate for American students. Also, this test covers ages 8-14 only; thus it is not appropriate for high school students.

Problem 4

A researcher is asked by school district personnel to collect data for a period of three years to determine whether their plans to improve third-grade reading skills are successful. The researcher decides to administer the same reading achievement test at the end of each school year for the next three years. List the aspects of their content that she should judge carefully as she examines various achievement tests for possible use in the study..

Sample Answer:

   a.   The degree of similarity between the content of the achievement test and the content of the district's third-grade reading curriculum.

   b.   The extent to which the content of the achievement test is up to date and reflects the students' culture.

   c.   The extent to which the test is appropriate for testing fourth-, fifth-, and sixth-grade students.

   d.   Whether the test ceiling is sufficiently high.

Problem 5

(Note to the instructor: This is a complex problem that might be assigned as a long homework assignment. See also problem 6 below, which is a simpler version of problem 5.)

   a.   Select one standardized test. If your thesis or dissertation will involve the use of standardized tests, select a measure relevant to that study. Otherwise, select a measure that relates to your major professional interests.

   b.   Obtain a specimen set for your measure. Most departments of psychology, university libraries, or counseling centers have a file of standardized tests. A copy of the test, the test manual, and the scoring key are included for most measures. Your instructor will give you the information you need to obtain a specimen set.

(Note to the instructor: If specimen sets are not available, you should make a collection of standard test catalogs and have students order the tests they will evaluate. These orders should be sent during the *first* week of the class so that they will arrive by the time they are needed. Some tests are restricted, and the student order will have to be endorsed by you.)

c. Sources of Information

   (1) Look up the selected measure in the most recent edition of the *Mental Measurements Yearbook* available in your institution's library. If your measure is not reviewed, select another measure.

   (2) Check the name of the measure you have selected in the most recent three annual volumes of *Psychological Abstracts* and ERIC's *CIJE* and *RIE*.. Also check key words related to the topic of the measure. For example, if your measure were the *IPAT Anxiety Scale Questionnaire*, you would check the key word *anxiety* in the subject index. Locate one study in which the measure was used. Read the study, giving particular attention to data related to the questions below. Prepare a note card on the article and submit it as part of this assignment.

d. Answer the following questions based on your study of the sources mentioned above.

   (1) Objectivity

      (a) Is the measure subject to administrator bias? Discuss.

      (b) Is the measure subject to scoring bias? Discuss.

   (2) Normative Data

      (a) Are normative data provided? Describe.

      (b) Are the samples used in establishing the norms satisfactory? Describe.

      (c) How comparable are norm groups to the sample in your study (if this measure is being considered for your thesis or dissertation project)?

   (3) Validity

      (a) What type of validity is most appropriate for this measure? Why?

      (b) What validity data are given in your sources? Describe.

      (c) Write a brief evaluation of the validity data available on this measure.

   (4) Reliability

      (a) What type of reliability data are available for this measure? Describe.

      (b) What are the reliability coefficients?

      (c) Write a brief evaluation of the reliability data available for this measure.

e. Submit a typed, double-spaced paper giving the name and a brief description of the measure, including the publisher's name, publication data, administration time, age levels if appropriate, and the types of scores that it yields. Answer the questions listed in d above. Be sure to include your note card with your paper [see (c-2)]. Be prepared to report on your standardized test evaluation in class. Turn in this form with your assignment.

Sample Answer:

Because each student is likely to select a different test to evaluate, it is not meaningful to provide a sample answer. You can award or deduct points for each part of the answer depending on its completeness and accuracy.

Problem 6
(Note to the instructor: This is a simpler version of problem 5.)
Find a test that pertains to a research problem or topic of interest to you in one of the sources listed in the annotated references (the section entitled *"Locating Information about Tests"*) for chapter 7 in the textbook. Indicate in writing:
  a. how the test possibly is relevant to your research problem.
  b. the reference source in which you identified the information.
  c. something interesting you learned about the test from the reference source. (Write just two sentences.)
Attach a copy of the page(s) in the reference source that reviews the test. (If the review is more than two pages, just copy the first two pages.) Write a complete, standard citation for the source on the first page of your copy.
Sample Answer:
Because each student is likely to select a different test to evaluate, it is not meaningful to provide a sample answer. You can award or deduct points for each part of the answer depending on its completeness and accuracy.

TEACHING ACTIVITIES

Activity 1
If you require students to do Application Problems 5 or 6, have them share their experiences in class. Ask them, What did you learn from doing this exercise? What problems did you encounter? What are the strengths and weaknesses of the test that you described?

Activity 2
Engage students in a discussion of this issue: Many educators believe that the most important things in education cannot be measured. Drawing on what you read in chapter 7, create a case supporting or criticizing this position.

Activity 3
Have students take all or part of an achievement test, attitude scale, or personality measure in class. Ask students to describe their experience in taking the test and what they learned from this experience that might affect the way they would administer the same or a similar test to a research sample.

Activity 4

Of the various standardized tests, projective techniques such as the *Rorschach* or the *Thematic Apperception Test* probably are most applicable to qualitative research because they assess how individuals view reality. If you can obtain a few cards from one of these tests, you can have students generate their own responses to them. You then can ask students to reflect on this experience and to consider how such tests might be used in educational research.

Activity 5

Before class, have students read a research article in which the study being reported used standardized tests. In class, have students discuss the tests and the types of information about the tests that were included in the report. Ask them to consider whether the tests were appropriate and whether adequate validity and reliability evidence was presented.

CHAPTER 8
COLLECTING RESEARCH DATA WITH
QUESTIONNAIRES AND INTERVIEWS

Note: The phrase in parentheses following the item number for both closed-form and open-form items, for example, 1. (obj. 3), refers to the textbook chapter objective to which the item is keyed.

CLOSED-FORM ITEMS

1. (obj. 1) The interview technique is better than a questionnaire when
    a. a small sample is adequate.
    b. in-depth responses are desired.
    c. factual information must be obtained.
    d. cost is a major consideration.
Answer: b

2. (obj. 1) An advantage of questionnaires over interviews is that questionnaires
    a. allow more flexibility in administration and in response.
    b. can be designed to require less subjective responses, thus minimizing bias.
    c. permit greater depth of response.
    d. are likely to yield more data on negative aspects of the respondents.
Answer: b

3. (obj. 2) Research has shown that when respondents receive questionnaires dealing with topics of great concern to them,
    a. respondents provide more biased data.
    b. more follow-ups are necessary to obtain a satisfactory response rate.
    c. respondents are less responsive to personal appeals to participate.
    d. the response rate is higher.
Answer: d

4. (obj. 2) Which of the following statements (all to be answered on a scale measuring degree of agreement or disagreement) is best constructed according to the rules for constructing questionnaire items?
   a. Every teacher should have several well-defined interests.
   b. Although unions are important in industry, they are inappropriate in education.
   c. Grouping students on the basis of ability provides for maximum attention to individual needs.
   d. Forcing students to take driver education is contrary to individual freedom.

Answer: c

5. (obj. 2) A rule that should be observed in constructing questionnaire items is to
   a. avoid predetermining how you will report the results of an item.
   b. be sure to use precise, technical language.
   c. avoid questions that require subjects to respond to two separate ideas in a single answer.
   d. use open-form items whenever possible.

Answer: c

6. (obj. 2) An important rule in designing a questionnaire is to
   a. use black ink on white paper.
   b. randomize item order.
   c. provide examples to explain potentially confusing items.
   d. put important items near the end of the questionnaire.

Answer: c

7. (obj. 3) Which of the following is a serious problem in using an anonymous questionnaire?
   a. Follow-ups are difficult and inefficient.
   b. No subgroup analyses can be performed.
   c. Respondents answer less thoughtfully and completely than on signed questionnaires.
   d. Respondents do not make a serious effort to answer accurately.

Answer: a

8. (obj. 4) The major advantage of closed-form questionnaire items over open-form questionnaire items is that closed-form items
   a. yield data that are more easily analyzed.
   b. are easier to design.
   c. are more valid.
   d. are less threatening.

Answer: a

9. (obj. 5) When attitude or opinion questions are asked on a questionnaire, it has been found that
   a. some respondents give opinions on topics about which they know nothing.
   b. uninformed responses can be eliminated by adding a "no opinion" choice.
   c. most attitudes can be satisfactorily measured with one well-phrased item.
   d. open-form attitude items usually provide more valid data.

Answer: a

10. (obj. 6) An important benefit of precontacting respondents before sending a questionnaire is that it
   a. encourages respondents to be more truthful in answering questionnaire items.
   b. permits respondents to decline to participate.
   c. increases the proportion of questionnaire recipients who complete the questionnaire.
   d. all of the above.

Answer: c

11. (obj. 7) It is essential that letters of transmittal for a questionnaire survey
   a. be individually typed.
   b. not refer to the respondent's institutional affiliation.
   c. specify when the questionnaire needs to be returned.
   d. include an explicit payment for the respondent's time.

Answer: c

12. (obj. 7) Which of the following guidelines should be followed in preparing the letter of transmittal for a mailed questionnaire?
   a. Refer to the respondent's affiliation with a group relevant to the questionnaire's topic.
   b. Avoid the use of appeals to the respondent's interest in doing good.
   c. Explain why the results of the questionnaire study cannot be made available to the respondents.
   d. Provide a summary of the literature that supports the study's objectives.

Answer: a

13. (obj. 8) If more than 20 percent of the questionnaires are not returned after several follow-up attempts, the researcher should
   a.   send another copy of the questionnaire to the nonrespondents.
   b.   select an additional sample and mail them the questionnaire.
   c.   interview a small random sample from the nonresponding group.
   d.   discontinue attempts to contact nonrespondents.
Answer: c

14. (obj. 8) On average, making three follow-up contacts with nonrespondents is likely to increase the response rate to a questionnaire by approximately ___ percent.
   a.   10
   b.   25
   c.   40
   d.   50
Answer: c

15. (obj. 9) The first step in conducting a study that will employ interviews to collect research data is to
   a.   specify how the data will be analyzed.
   b.   train interviewers.
   c.   select a sample.
   d.   define the purpose of the interview.
Answer: d

16. (obj. 10) Key informants tend to differ from other members of the defined population in all but which one of the following ways?
   a.   Their possession of a unique perspective on the phenomenon of interest to the researcher.
   b.   Greater knowledge about the phenomenon being investigated.
   c.   Better ability to communicate with the researcher about the phenomenon.
   d.   Possession of the emic perspective concerning the phenomenon.
Answer: d

17. (obj. 10) An interview that seeks to learn how informants structure their social or physical world is called
    a.   a confirmation survey interview.
    b.   a participant construct interview.
    c.   a projective technique interview.
    d.   a key informant interview.
Answer: b

18. (obj. 11) The first question that the interviewer asks each respondent is, "Do you think parents should be able to send their child to any school in the city, should only send their child to the school nearest their home, or should pay a special fee if they wish their child to attend a school other than the one in their neighborhood?" This question is typical of those asked in
    a.   an unstructured interview.
    b.   a structured interview.
    c.   a standardized open-ended interview.
    d.   an informal conversational interview.
Answer: b

19. (obj. 11) In an unstructured interview, the interviewer tends to
    a.   follow a general plan that allows the individual to respond freely.
    b   not have predetermined objectives.
    c.   not take notes or record the interview.
    d.   use structured questions to probe more deeply.
Answer: a

20. (obj. 12) A major advantage of conducting telephone interviews with the aid of a computer is that
    a.   it prevents the interviewer from rephrasing questions.
    b.   a live interviewer is not needed to ask the questions.
    c.   the computer can be programmed to detect when a respondent is lying.
    d.   the computer indicates the next appropriate question based on the previous response.
Answer: d

21. (obj. 12) An important disadvantage of telephone interviewing as compared with face-to-face interviewing is that
   a. telephone interviewing is more costly.
   b. there is more likelihood that the interviewer will fake data in telephone interviews.
   c. frequent call-backs become very expensive if no one answers the phone.
   d. only persons with telephones can be reached.
Answer: d

22. (obj. 12) Research comparisons of telephone and face-to-face interviews have found that
   a. telephone interviews cannot be used to collect sensitive data.
   b. about twice as many face-to-face interviews are completed.
   c. telephone interviews are much easier to monitor and supervise.
   d. about 20 percent of U.S. households do not have telephones, thus leading to biased samples.
Answer: c

23. (obj. 13) An essential criterion for selecting interviewers to conduct research interviews is to select
   a. males to interview male respondents and females to interview female respondents.
   b. interviewers who are older than the respondents.
   c. interviewers who are members of the respondent target population.
   d. interviewers who are able to relate to the respondents positively.
Answer: d

24. (obj. 14) An important purpose of the interview guide when a study involves several interviewers is to
   a. train interviewers in question wording, format, recording procedures, and allowable probes.
   b. serve as a script from which interviewers can read when asking questions during the interview.
   c. provide information for answering any queries from respondents about the research hypotheses.
   d. all of the above.
Answer: a

25. (obj. 14) In preparing interviewers to use an interview guide, the researcher should
    a. avoid informing the interviewers about the study's hypotheses and research questions.
    b. inform the interviewers about the study's hypotheses and research questions, and provide the rationale for each one.
    c. allow the interviewers to use their natural interviewing style rather than training them to standardize their use of the interview guide.
    d. focus on general principles of interviewing rather than on the specific aspects of the interview guide.
Answer: a

26. (obj. 15) In her interview notes the interviewer comments on the respondent's speech pacing and pauses during the interview. These notes   reflect the interviewer's attention to the task of
    a. understanding the respondent's language and culture.
    b. being sensitive to nonverbal information.
    c. gaining the respondent's trust.
    d. appearing competent in the eyes of the respondent.
Answer: b

27. (obj. 15) An essential task of the interviewer during a research interview is to
    a. record word-for-word each of the respondent's comments.
    b. help the respondent feel comfortable in the interview situation.
    c. clarify the interviewer's own experiences and beliefs concerning the research topic.
    d. avoid taking notes so as not to distract the respondent.
Answer: b

28. (obj. 16) The chief advantage of note taking during an interview is that it
    a. provides the most accurate possible record of the subject's responses.
    b. speeds up the interview process.
    c. enhances the respondents' concentration.
    d. provides readily accessible data for analysis.
Answer: d

29. (obj. 16) Tape recording an interview generally
    a. requires the interviewer himself to evaluate and classify the responses.
    b. reduces any tendency of the interviewer to bias the data.
    c puts respondents on the defensive.
    d. eliminates the option of anonymity.
Answer: b

30. (obj. 17) To analyze responses to open-form interview questions, quantitative researchers typically
   a. calculate the number of times that particular words are uttered by each respondent.
   b. replay a tape recording of the interview.
   c. develop a category system to code the responses.
   d. have two or more raters rate the responses of each respondent.

Answer: c

OPEN-FORM ITEMS

1. (obj. 1) Give at least two advantages and two disadvantages of the use of interviews compared to the use of questionnaires in a research study.

Answer (any 2 from each set OK):

Advantages
   a. The interview is more flexible and adaptable; the interviewer can follow up leads.
   b. The interview permits greater depth of response.
   c. The interview yields more complete data.
   d. The interview yields more data on negative aspects of the subjects.
   e. The interview provides data more appropriate for qualitative analysis.

Disadvantages
   a. The interview is more costly and time-consuming to administer.
   b. The interview is more subjective and thus subject to bias.
   c. The interview cannot provide anonymity for the respondents.
   d. Subjects may become embarrassed in a face-to-face situation.
   e. It is difficult to sample respondents from a widely distributed geographic area.

2. (obj. 2) Describe one desirable procedure for pretesting a questionnaire for use in a research study.

Answer (any 1 OK):
   a. Leave space on the questionnaire for respondents to state what they think each question means.
   b. Do in-depth interviews with a sample of respondents to solicit their interpretations of the questions.
   c. Try different versions of specific questions on different subgroups of the pretest sample.
   d. Revise the items based on the above steps and then submit the revised questionnaire to another pretest sample to test the response rate.

3. (obj. 2) Briefly identify two of the major steps involved in carrying out a research study based on a questionnaire.
Answer (any 2 OK):
   a. Defining the objectives for the questionnaire.
   b. Selecting the sample.
   c. Designing the questionnaire format.
   d. Pretesting the questionnaire.
   e. Precontacting the sample.
   f. Writing a cover letter and distributing the questionnaire.
   g. Following up with nonrespondents.
   h. Analyzing the questionnaire data.

4. (obj. 3) Describe one procedure that can be used to provide anonymity to questionnaire respondents.
Answer (any 1 OK):
   a. Create a master code sheet that contains a code for each individual in the sample; put the codes on the questionnaires; and when a questionnaire is returned, check off the name of the person having that code on the master code sheet.
   b. Send each individual a prepaid postcard with the code on it, and a questionnaire that contains no code; ask the individual to return the questionnaire and the postcard separately.

5. (obj. 4) Describe the difference between an open-form and a closed-form question, and identify which form usually is preferable for collecting qualitative information and why.
Answer:
An open-form question permits the subject to respond in his own words; for example, essay questions are open-form. A closed form-question permits only certain responses, for example, a multiple-choice item. An open-form format is preferable for collecting qualitative information because it permits respondents to respond at any length and in their own terms, consistent with the principles of qualitative research.

6. (obj. 5) Describe one strategy that can be used to reduce the tendency for questionnaire respondents to give opinions about attitude objects with which they are unfamiliar.
Answer (any 1 OK):
   a. Include a "no opinion" response option for each item.
   b. Include several information questions at the beginning of the questionnaire to screen out respondents who lack knowledge about the attitude object.
   c. Select your sample from a population of individuals who are likely to have a sufficient level of knowledge about the attitude object, e.g., college-educated people.

7. (obj. 6) Describe one advantage of precontacting the sample to whom you plan to send a questionnaire.
Answer (any 1 OK):

    a.   A precontact alerts respondents to expect the questionnaire, so they are less likely to disregard it by mistake.

    b.   A precontact puts a more personal, human face on the research study, which might make participants more comfortable and also more willing to reveal personal information honestly.

    c.   If the precontact obtains respondents' commitment to participate, they are likely to feel obligated to keep their commitment when the questionnaire arrives.

8. (obj. 7) Describe three features that can be incorporated in a letter of transmittal for a mailed questionnaire to make it effective.
Answer (any 3 OK):

    a.   The use of mail-merge on a word processor to personalize the addresses.

    b.   Duplication of the letter by using a word processor or offset process so that the letter appears individually typed.

    c.   A brief description of the study's purpose.

    d.   Emphasis on the study's importance.

    e.   Mention of the value of obtaining this respondent's views.

    f.   A reasonable, but specific, time within which to return the questionnaire.

    g.   Enclosing a self-addressed, stamped envelope (SASE) to make the return convenient.

    h.   Assurance of the confidentiality of the information to be obtained.

    i.   An offer to share a summary of the results if the respondent is interested.

    j.   Expression of appreciation for the respondent's cooperation, time, etc.

    k.   Personal signing of the letter or printing of the signature in a different color.

    l.   Sending the letter from an individual whose endorsement represents a favorable symbol of authority.

9. (obj. 8) A researcher received 72 percent of the questionnaires that were sent to a sample of high school counselors. Describe one method the researcher could use to increase the response rate.
Answer:

    a.   Send a different follow-up letter with another copy of the questionnaire.

    b.   Telephone nonrespondents and ask them to return the questionnaire.

    c.   Send a telegram to nonrespondents, asking them to return the questionnaire.

    d.   Send a postcard reminder asking nonrespondents to return the questionnaire.

10. (obj. 9) Briefly list three steps involved in doing a research project with interviews as the means of collecting data.
Answer (any 3 OK):
   a. Defining the purpose of the study.
   b. Selecting a sample.
   c. Designing the interview format.
   d. Developing questions.
   e. Selecting and training interviewers.
   f. Pilot-testing the interview procedures.
   g. Conducting the interviews.
   h. Analyzing the interview data.

11. (obj. 10) What is a key informant interview?
Answer:
An interview in which the interviewer collects data from individuals who have special knowledge or perceptions that would not be available to the researcher from other individuals in the defined population or in the field setting.

12. (obj. 10) Describe one of the defining characteristics of a focus group as used in educational research.
Answer (any 1 OK):
   a. It involves group discussion of a defined topic.
   b. It provides a permissive, nonthreatening environment in which informants can express their views.
   c. It is conducted with about 7-10 people by a skilled interviewer.
   d. Group members may influence one another by responding to others' ideas and comments.

13. (obj. 11) Describe the format of each of the following types of interviews used in qualitative research: (a) the informal conversational interview, (b) the general interview guide approach, and (c) the standardized open-ended interview.
Answer:

    a.   The informal conversational interview relies entirely on the spontaneous generation of questions in a natural interaction; a participant may not even realize that she is being interviewed, because the interviewer engages in a seemingly casual conversation with her.

    b.   In the general interview guide approach, the interviewer has a standard outline of a set of topics to be explored with each respondent; topics can be explored in varied order and questions can be worded differently depending on how the interview evolves.

    c.   In the standardized open-ended interview, the interviewer asks a predetermined set of questions of each respondent in the same sequence and with the same wording.

14. (obj. 12) Describe two advantages of conducting interviews by telephone rather than in person.
Answer (any 2 OK):

    a.   Respondents can be selected from a much broader accessible population because there is no need for the interviewers to travel to the location of each respondent.

    b.   Because all interviewers can work from a central location, monitoring of interviews and quality control are much easier.

    c.   In telephone interviewing little cost is incurred when no one answers, making frequent call-backs feasible.

    d.   Many groups such as business people, school personnel, and parents are easier to reach by telephone than by personal visits.

    e.   Telephone interviewing provides safe access to dangerous locations, and access to restricted locations where interviewers might not be admitted.

    f.   Telephone interviews are less expensive than face-to-face interviews, especially when the sample is geographically dispersed.

15. (obj. 12) Describe one common problem in interview research that computer-assisted telephone interviewing virtually eliminates.
Answer (any 1 OK):

    a.   Data can be recorded in the wrong place on the interview response form.

    b.   The interviewer can ask the wrong question after a given response.

    c.   It may take a long time to transfer the interview data to a form in which they can be statistically analyzed.

16. (obj. 13) Describe one selection criterion that researchers often establish in selecting the interviewers for a research study.

Answer (any 1 OK):

   a.   Matching interviewers and respondents on critical variables (e.g., social class, race, age, or gender).

   b.   Selecting interviewers who are members of the respondent's target population.

   c.   Retaining only interviewers who during training meet criterion standards of performance.

17. (obj. 14) Briefly describe the two phases in the training of research interviewers.

Answer:

   a.   The trainees study the interview guide to learn about question wording, format, recording procedures, and allowable probes, and they also are informed about the interview conditions (e.g., logistics, necessary controls and safeguards, and topics being investigated).

   b.   The trainees conduct practice interviews and receive corrective feedback until their performance becomes polished and reaches the desired level of structure, objectivity, and reliability.

18. (obj. 15) State one circumstance in which superficial rapport with the interview respondent is sufficient and one circumstance in which the interviewer needs to develop stronger rapport.

Answer:

Superficial rapport is sufficient when the respondent already appears very comfortable with the interview process. Stronger rapport is needed when the interviewer intends to ask the respondent to reveal sensitive or deeply personal information.

19. (obj. 16) List one advantage and one disadvantage of note taking as a method of recording interview responses as compared to tape recording the interview.

Answer (any 1 from each set OK):

   Advantages

   a.   When notes are taken during or immediately after the interview, it is not necessary for anyone to listen to a tape and transcribe the interview
before beginning the data analysis.

   b.   The presence of a tape recorder may distract or upset some respondents.

   Disadvantages

   a.   The interviewer cannot simply listen but must pause to take notes, which can disrupt communication.

   b.   The interviewer may forget to make a record of some important information.

   c.   There is no opportunity to check the accuracy of the record of the respondent's answers or to reanalyze the data at a later time.

20. (obj. 17) How does a researcher typically analyze the responses to closed-form interview or questionnaire items?

Answer:
The researcher calculates the percentage of respondents who indicated each response option for each item.

APPLICATION PROBLEMS

Problem 1
Give an example of the type of information for which using only one item on a questionnaire would be suitable and an example of a type of information for which using only one item on a questionnaire would not be suitable.

Sample Answer:
One item on a questionnaire is suitable for seeking the answer to a specific fact, e.g., asking a teacher how many students in her first-period class have been absent ten days or more so far during the school year. To collect information about attitudes--for example, to learn how students feel about their school's policy for handling incidents of violence--the researcher needs to use an attitude scale that includes several items in order to obtain a reliable assessment of their attitudes.

Problem 2
A researcher wants to learn the factors that determine where college students decide to live while attending a university. State one question that typifies what a quantitative researcher might ask in interviewing students on this topic and one that typifies what a qualitative researcher might ask.

Sample Answer:
Quantitative researchers generally prespecify the variables of interest in the research and thus ask specific questions, e.g., "Did your parents influence your decision as to where to live this year while at the university?"
Qualitative researchers typically do not prespecify the aspects of the phenomena that interest them and so ask broad questions, e.g., "How did you decide where to live this year while at the university?"

Problem 3

A researcher is studying the unique needs of physically challenged students during the school day. Name two types of individual who could serve as a key informants for the researcher.

Sample Answer:

Teachers who have one or more severely physically challenged students in their classes would be key informants. Students who have physical handicaps but who are not handicapped verbally or socially would also be key informants, as would the parents of such students.

TEACHING ACTIVITIES

Activity 1

Have students select a topic on which to collect information by interviewing or giving a brief questionnaire to several individuals. Provide class time to assist students in designing their questionnaires or interview guides. (If desired, students can work in groups.) You also can ask the students to design a procedure for obtaining feedback to be collected from the respondents about the effectiveness of the questionnaire or interview guides. Specify a date by which the data need to be collected. Give students the assignment of writing a brief report on the procedures used in, and the results obtained from, their questionnaires or interviews. Discuss some of the reports in class.

Activity 2

Locate a research report in which the researcher used either questionnaires or interviews as the method of collecting data. (Several recent studies are listed in the text at the beginning of chapter 8.) Have students use the guidelines for designing a questionnaire in figure 8.1 in the textbook, or for conducting a research interview in figure 8.5 in the textbook, to evaluate the information in the research report.

Activity 3

Bring to class a few cover letters that were used in questionnaire or interview studies conducted by you or your colleagues. Ask students to note which features of the sample cover letter in figure 8.2 in the textbook were addressed by each of the cover letters and to evaluate the overall effectiveness of each.

CHAPTER 9
COLLECTING RESEARCH DATA THROUGH
OBSERVATION AND CONTENT ANALYSIS

Note: The phrase in parentheses following the item number for both closed-form and open-form items, for example, 1. (obj. 3), refers to the textbook chapter objective to which the item is keyed.

CLOSED-FORM ITEMS

1. (obj. 1) A major advantage of observation over questionnaires is that observation
    a. is not susceptible to the self-report bias of questionnaires.
    b. requires less time for data collection and analysis.
    c. is not susceptible to theoretical saturation.
    d. needs to be employed only at one point in time in order to obtain reliable data.
Answer: a

2. (obj. 2) The number of students who enter a classroom after the lesson has started is an example of
    a. an inferential observational variable.
    b. an evaluative observational variable.
    c. a descriptive observational variable.
    d. a duration observational variable.
Answer: c

3. (obj. 2) Which of the following is an example of an inferential observational variable?
    a. the number of times an audience applauds during a lecture.
    b. the lecturer's empathy with the audience.
    c. the amount of time that the lecturer used an overhead projector.
    d. the quality of the examples provided by the lecturer.
Answer: b

4. (obj. 3) A researcher records whether a particular student is on-task or off-task when the lesson begins, five minutes later, and every five minutes thereafter until the lesson is over. This procedure for recording observations is called
    a. continuous recording.
    b. frequency-count recording.
    c. duration recording.
    d. interval recording.
Answer: d

5. (obj. 3) Measuring the elapsed time that target behaviors occur is referred to as
   a. duration recording.
   b. time sampling.
   c. interval recording.
   d. continuous observation.
Answer: d

6. (obj. 4) One disadvantage of using standard observation schedules to collect data is that
   a. they tend to have low reliability.
   b. typically it is not possible to find a schedule that includes all the variables that the researcher wishes to measure.
   c. they generally require a high level of inference.
   d. they are limited to frequency-count recording.
Answer: b

7. (obj. 5) Audiotape or videotape recording is especially useful in observational research when
   a. teacher-student interaction occurs with low frequency.
   b. descriptive variables are to be recorded.
   c. inter-rater reliability must be calculated.
   d. untrained observers are used.
Answer: c

8. (obj. 6) In the training of observers, it is desirable to
   a. show videotapes of events similar to those that will be observed during actual data collection.
   b. avoid the use of videotapes, because they do not provide the context needed for reliable observation.
   c. train each observer independently so that the observers do not bias one another.
   d. allow the observers to develop their own rules for resolving disagreements in recording events.
Answer: a

124

9. (obj. 8) The term *observer drift* refers to the tendency for observers to
    a. stop attending to the situation during long periods of recording observational data.
    b. decline in inter-rater reliability over time.
    c. use different standards for making ratings of groups toward whom they have a bias.
    d. gradually deviate from the standard definitions of observational variables that they learned during training.

Answer: d

10. (obj. 8) Observers who tend to rate most individuals at the high end of a scale are exhibiting
    a. the halo effect.
    b. the error of leniency.
    c. acquiescence.
    d. contamination.

Answer: b

11. (obj. 9) Which one of the following is *not* a characteristic of qualitative observation?
    a. The observer looks at events from a holistic perspective.
    b. The observer attempts to remain neutral during data collection.
    c. The observer can change the focus of observation as data collection proceeds.
    d. The observer is not constrained by prespecified hypotheses and variables.

Answer: b

12. (obj. 10) A researcher who became a substitute teacher in order to collect data about the culture of substitute teaching can be said to have assumed the role of
    a. an observer participant.
    b. a participant observer.
    c. a complete participant.
    d. an unobtrusive participant.

Answer: c

13. (obj. 11) In qualitative observation, the point at which the researcher decides that new observational findings are replicating earlier findings is called
    a. the focused stage.
    b. the reflective stage.
    c. grounded-theory replication.
    d. theoretical saturation.

Answer: d

14. (obj. 11) As data collection proceeds in qualitative observation, the researcher's observations are likely to become more
    a. focused.
    b. objective.
    c. reflective of the observer's role as complete participant.
    d. oriented to the study of material culture.
Answer: a

15. (obj. 12) To prepare for making field observations, a qualitative researcher should find it helpful to
    a. use the same training procedures as those used in quantitative observation.
    b. serve an apprenticeship with an experienced qualitative researcher.
    c. focus on achieving a high level of criterion-related observer reliability.
    d. focus on learning procedures to avoid reliability decay.
Answer: b

16. (obj. 13) Field notes in qualitative research should
    a. focus on theoretical constructs rather than on concrete details of the events being observed.
    b. focus on duration and frequency variables.
    c. never be made surreptitiously.
    d. include both descriptive details and the observer's reflections.
Answer: d

17. (obj. 14) In qualitative research, observer bias
    a. is best avoided by making video recordings of the events being studied.
    b. is best avoided by having someone other than the researcher who designed the study collect the data.
    c. can be reduced by using both quantitative and qualitative methods of data collection.
    d. is an issue only at the descriptive stage of data collection.
Answer: c

18. (obj. 15) A limitation of unobtrusive measures is that they
    a. alter the meaning of the variable that is being studied.
    b. are susceptible to response sets.
    c. are influenced by the observer's presence.
    d. have uncertain reliability.
Answer: d

19. (obj. 15) Unobtrusive measures have the advantage of
    a. requiring less time for data collection.
    b. not being susceptible to observer effects.
    c. permitting the researcher to study a total behavior pattern.
    d. not requiring the use of sampling techniques.
Answer: b

20. (obj. 15) Qualitative researchers
    a. study physical objects as expressions of how groups construct social reality.
    b. do not study physical objects, because they are decontextualized.
    c. study physical objects only if they can interview the individuals who constructed or used them.
    d. study only physical objects that have a communication function.
Answer: a

21. (obj. 16) The categories used to code documents in a quantitative content analysis
    a. must use a consistent unit of analysis, such as a sentence or a paragraph.
    b. must be derived directly from the documents rather than from the study's research objectives.
    c. should be checked to determine whether raters can use them to code documents reliably.
    d. all of the above.
Answer: c

22. (obj. 17) In qualitative research, the meaning of a document is assumed to
    a. reside in the minds of its author and of the individuals who read it.
    b. reside in a universal linguistic code.
    c. be invariant across readers.
    d. be invariant across time.
Answer: a

OPEN-FORM ITEMS

1. (obj. 1) State one advantage and one disadvantage of observation as a data-collection method in research.
Answer (any 1 from each set OK):
    Advantages
    a.   Observation avoids the bias often found in self-report data.
    b.   Observation does not depend on the verbal fluency of the research participants.
    Disadvantages
    a.   Some variables are difficult to observe and record.
    b.   Observer bias can occur.
    c.   The presence of the observer can change the situation being observed.
    d.   Observational data tend to be expensive and time-consuming to collect.

2. (obj. 2) An observer collects quantitative data about (a) the number of meetings that an administrator attends during one work week, (b) how effective the administrator is in each meeting, and (c) the extent to which the administrator employs participatory decision making. Classify each of these observational variables using the three classification categories presented in the textbook.
Answer:
    a.   Descriptive observational variable.
    b.   Evaluative observational variable.
    c.   Inferential observational variable.

3. (obj. 3) In recording observational variables in quantitative research, the researcher must decide whether to make a continuous recording or to use some other type of recording procedure. Name and briefly describe two other possible types of recording procedure.
Answer (any 2 OK):
    a.   Duration recording, which involves measuring the amount of time that each observational variable occurs.
    b.   Frequency recording, which involves counting each instance of the observational variable.
    c.   Interval recording, which involves checking for the occurrence of the observational variable at a regular interval.

4. (obj. 4) State at least one advantage and one disadvantage of using a standard observational schedule in a research project.
Answer (any 1 from each set OK):
   Advantages
   a.   Usually well developed, yielding valid and reliable data.
   b.   Saves the investigator all the time and effort required to develop her own schedule.
   c.   Permits comparing the findings with those of other researchers who used the same schedule.
   Disadvantages
   a.   The items may address some topics in which you are not interested.
   b.   The schedule may not cover all the areas about which you want information.

5. (obj. 5) State two tasks that a computer can perform when a researcher includes observational data in a research study.
Answer (any 2 OK):
   a.   Record and time events.
   b.   Transfer observational data into a computer file.
   c.   Detect coding errors.
   d.   Create graphic data displays of observational results.

6. (obj. 6) If observers disagree with one anothers' ratings while being trained to use an observational schedule, what is one procedure that the researcher can use to resolve the disagreement?
Answer (any 1 OK):
   a.   Review the event that the disagreement involved and explain how it should be recorded.
   b.   Revise the definition of variables on the observation schedule to remove ambiguities that may have caused the disagreement.
   c.   Write data-recording rules to handle the situation that caused the disagreement.

7. (obj. 7) Describe a procedure that a researcher could use to check the inter-rater reliability of three observers who will collect data on 20 meetings of a university faculty senate.
Answer:
Have all three observers together attend a certain number of the meetings and collect data on the same observational variables. Determine the extent to which the observers' ratings agree with one anothers' by calculating the appropriate inter-rater reliability statistic.

8. (obj. 8) A common error in making quantitative observations involving ratings is the error of leniency. Describe two other rating errors that occur in quantitative observation.

    a.   The error of central tendency, which occurs when the observer rates most of the research participants near the middle of the rating scale. This error occurs because the observer is unable to discriminate between the behavior of different participants.

    b.   The halo effect, which occurs when the observer forms an opinion of a research participant based on information about the participant on one variable and then allows this information to influence her ratings of the participant on other variables.

9. (obj. 9) Explain one major difference between observation in quantitative research and observation in qualitative research.

Answer (any 1 OK):

    a.   In quantitative research, observers attempt to remain objective (i.e., neutral) about the phenomena being studied. In qualitative research, observers consider their personal reactions and reflections to be part of the phenomena being studied.

    b.   In quantitative research, observers collect data about prespecified variables. In qualitative research, observers can change the aspect of the phenomenon about which data are to be collected as the study proceeds.

    c.   The focus of observation in qualitative research typically is much wider and includes more aspects of context than in quantitative research.

10. (obj. 10) A qualitative researcher who is studying a private Christian school participates in many of its activities as a volunteer, for example, by serving as a teacher aide, driving the school bus, and cleaning up after church services. The observer is of a different faith than those in the school community. What type of observational role is the researcher performing?

Answer:

The researcher is a participant observer.

11. (obj. 11) What typically occurs during the focused stage of observation in a qualitative research study?

Answer:

The observer collects more intensive data about the features of the phenomenon that proved to be of most interest during the descriptive stage.

12. (obj. 12) While a qualitative researcher is in the process of collecting observational data, an expert advises him to change his data-collection procedures. Is it acceptable for the researcher to make the recommended changes, and why?
Answer:
Yes, in qualitative research, observational methods can be changed as the researcher develops new insights.

13. (obj. 13) A qualitative researcher wishes to make notes about what she is observing in a field situation but does not wish to be seen doing so. How can the researcher deal with this situation?
Answer:
The researcher may be able to make a few notes surreptitiously in the field setting or write a summary of what she observed immediately upon leaving the setting. These few notes or the summary can be expanded into a more complete set of field notes at a later time.

14. (obj. 14) Suppose the individuals being observed appear to be affected by the observer's presence. Compare how a qualitative researcher and a quantitative researcher would handle this situation.
Answer:
The qualitative researcher would collect and analyze data about the individuals' reactions to his presence. In contrast, the quantitative researcher would not collect any data until the individuals had appeared to have adjusted to his presence.

15. (obj. 15) How might computer printouts generated by trainees in an architectural drafting firm be studied (a) by a quantitative researcher as unobtrusive measures and (b) by a qualitative researcher as objects of material culture?
Answer:
    a.   The quantitative researcher would obtain permission to collect the printouts without the knowledge of the trainees or their supervisor. The printouts would be analyzed by using prespecified variables.
    b.   The qualitative researcher would study the printouts as expressions of how individuals and groups construct a material culture that has certain purposes, including the communication of information. The qualitative researcher also would be interested in the symbolic meanings of the computer printouts and the contexts in which they are used.

16. (objs. 16-17) How would a quantitative researcher and a qualitative researcher differ in their approach to analyzing the content of a textbook?

Answer:

The quantitative researcher would code the content by using categories that reflect prespecified variables. The frequency of occurrence of each category most likely would be determined. In contrast, a qualitative researcher would study the meaning of the text for the author and for different audiences with no preconceived variables in mind. Also a qualitative researcher would be more likely to study contextual features relating to the textbook (e.g., the situations in which students read it) than would a quantitative researcher.

APPLICATION PROBLEMS

Problem 1

A researcher is interested in testing the theory that children learn by imitating the behavior of others. To test the theory, she asks one group of teachers to be exceptionally neat in their classrooms for a period of several weeks, for example, conspicuously taking time to arrange their desks (i.e., the teacher's own desk in the classroom) neatly. She asks another group of teachers to be sloppy for a similar period of time. The researcher's prediction is that children whose teachers are neat will themselves be neater by the end of the experiment than will children whose teachers are sloppy. What is one unobtrusive measure of the children's degree of neatness that could be used in this experiment?

Sample Answer:

a. The extent to which the objects in the children's desks are organized in an orderly manner.

b. The amount of litter on the floor at the end of the school day.

c. The neatness of the children's paperwork.

d. If there is an area for storing coats during the school day, the neatness with which the children's clothes are arranged in it.

e. The alignment of the students' desks in an orderly pattern at the end of the school day.

Problem 2

A researcher wants to determine whether the thought level of students' essays improves from the first to the fourth year of college. She has a collection of essays written by the same students over a four-year period of college attendance. What are three aspects of essay-writing style that could be content-analyzed to yield a measure of thought level?

Sample Answer:
a. Frequency of the use of low-frequency words.
b. Frequency of words denoting abstract concepts, e.g., *nationalism, logic, symbolism*.
c. Frequency of connectives such as *if, but, therefore*, and *whereas*.
d. Average length of sentences.
e. Frequency of cited evidence in support of a position.

Problem 3

A quantitative researcher and a qualitative researcher want to use observational methods to study the phenomenon of collegiality among the counselors and other service staff in a high school. How are the two researchers likely to differ in (a) their approach to conceptualizing collegiality and (b) the types of data that they would collect?

Sample Answer:
a. The quantitative researcher would identify observable aspects of collegiality, would conceptualize each aspect as a separate variable, and would develop an observation schedule for recording data on each variable. The qualitative researcher would do less conceptualization prior to collecting data in the field. His emerging conceptualization would focus on the different meanings of collegiality for individuals in different roles (e.g., counselors, speech therapists, and nurses) and on the context in which collegiality is manifested.

b. The quantitative researcher would collect numerical data on variables that are descriptive, inferential, or evaluative. The qualitative researcher would collect verbal data, and perhaps visual data as well, about collegiality and the context in which it occurs and does not occur. The qualitative researcher's data would be rather general at the descriptive stage of data collection, and in the focused and selected stages it would narrow to fewer elements in the situation with more intensive data being collected about each element.

Problem 4

A quantitative researcher and a qualitative researcher are working as members of a team project whose goal is to study how journeymen contractors work with apprentice construction workers to guide their learning of their trades. While training observers, the quantitative researcher finds out that some of them bias their observational ratings in favor of contractors who were originally trained as carpenters. Upon hearing of this bias, the qualitative researcher realizes that she, too, shares their bias that contractors with a carpentry background are more effective than those with another construction specialization (e.g., electricians, cabinet makers, or painters). How would each researcher be likely to deal with this bias?

Sample Answer:

a. The quantitative researcher would eliminate observers from the study if their bias continues to affect their ratings despite training in the observational schedule. Also, the researcher would take care not to reveal to the observers whether the contractors to be observed were originally trained as carpenters or in some other construction specialization.

b. The qualitative researcher would check whether her bias affected her findings by making active efforts to test rival explanations for the findings, using both qualitative and quantitative research methods, using multiple observers, and examining the findings from various theoretical perspectives.

TEACHING ACTIVITIES

Activity 1

Assign students to read a quantitative research study and a qualitative research study that involves the use of observational methods. In class, have students compare how the observational data were collected, analyzed, and reported in the two studies.

Activity 2

If you know a researcher who is doing or has done a quantitative or a qualitative research study involving extensive observation, invite this person to be a guest presenter. Ask the researcher to discuss why he chose to collect observational data, how he prepared to collect such data, any problems he experienced while collecting the data, and how the data were analyzed.

Activity 3
You can demonstrate the complexity of making field notes or doing continuous recording by showing a few minutes of a video recording of a classroom lesson or other educational event. As the event is being shown, ask students to write down everything that they observe. You can ask some of the students to write their notes on a transparency, so that they can be shared with others in the class by showing them on an overhead projector. Ask students what they learned about collecting observational data from this experience.

Activity 4
Mention a complex construct such as enthusiasm, attentiveness, or empathy. Ask students to identify observable indicators of the construct and how these indicators might be recorded in a quantitative research study.

CHAPTER 10
DESCRIPTIVE AND CAUSAL-COMPARATIVE RESEARCH DESIGNS

Note: The phrase in parentheses following the item number for both closed-form and open-form items, for example, 1. (obj. 3), refers to the textbook chapter objective to which the item is keyed.

CLOSED-FORM ITEMS

1. (obj. 1) In educational research, description
   a. is a major goal of both quantitative and qualitative research.
   b. rarely is the focus of data-collection efforts.
   c. is associated with nonparametric tests of statistical significance.
   d. focuses on demonstrating cause-effect connections.

Answer: a

2. (obj. 1) Causal-comparative research differs most distinctly from descriptive research in its
   a. use of measures of central tendency and measures of variability.
   b. appropriateness for exploring how variables are related to each other.
   c. potential for impact on educational practice.
   d. study of the same population at different times.

Answer: b

3. (obj. 2) A descriptive research study would be likely to report all but which of the following types of scores or statistics?
   a. Standard deviation.
   b. Mean.
   c. Percentiles.
   d. Analysis of variance.

Answer: d

4. (obj. 3) An opinion poll is an example of which type of descriptive research?
   a. Description of a sample at one point in time.
   b. Cross-sectional research.
   c. Longitudinal research.
   d. Case study research.

Answer: a

5. (obj. 4) Longitudinal research is particularly useful for studying
   a. the development of individuals.
   b. differences in the characteristics of individuals who vary in age.
   c. possible causal relationships between different variables.
   d. differences in the views of various members of a defined population at a given time.
Answer: a

6. (obj. 4) If a researcher studies the same population over time by repeatedly contacting the same sample of individuals, the researcher is conducting a ___ study.
   a. trend
   b. cohort
   c. panel
   d. cross-sectional
Answer: c

7. (obj. 4) Match each of the following types of longitudinal research study with the appropriate description of what audience is studied at each data-collection point.
   __ 1. Trend study.
   __ 2. Cohort study.
   __ 3. Panel study.
   a. A different sample from a population that changes over time.
   b. A different sample from the same population.
   c. The entire population.
   d. The same sample from the same population.
Answer: 1=a, 2=b, 3=d

8. (obj. 5) Compared with a longitudinal study, an important advantage of a cross-sectional study is that
   a. information is collected at several points in time.
   b. the data can be obtained more rapidly.
   c. developmental changes can be detected more accurately.
   d. the data are not distorted by faulty recall.
Answer: b

9. (obj. 5) Suppose you wish to examine the changes in attitudes toward school that occur as students mature. You select a sample of elementary school, middle school, and high school students and measure their attitudes toward school. A weakness of your cross-sectional design for studying this research problem is that
    a. this method cannot be used to explore relationships between variables.
    b. this method cannot be used to explore developmental changes.
    c. the sample of elementary, middle, and high school students may differ on other characteristics besides grade level.
    d. data must be collected over an extended time period.
Answer: c

10. (obj. 6) Match each of the following research results with the type of interpretation of it that a researcher is likely to make about the relationship among females' athletic participation (X), engaging in irresponsible sexual activity (Y), and receiving supportive parenting (Z).
    __ 1. Female students who participate in school athletic events are less likely to engage in irresponsible sexual activity.
    __ 2. Females with supportive parents are more likely to participate in athletic events while in school and to make responsible decisions about sexual activity.
    __ 3. Females who engage in irresponsible sexual activity have less time and interest for athletic participation while in school.
    a. Z causes both X and Y.
    b. Y causes X.
    c. X causes Y.
    Answers: 1=c, 2=a, 3=b

11. (obj. 6) In causal-comparative research, matching is used to
    a. equate two groups on one or more extraneous variables.
    b. identify groups that represent the extremes of a phenomenon.
    c. predict the direction of a presumed causal relationship.
    d. describe the characteristics of two groups.
Answer: a

12. (obj. 7) The best way to select two groups for comparison in a causal-comparative research study so that they are highly different in the presumed causal variable is
   a. through the use of matching.
   b. by random selection of the groups from the defined population.
   c. by determining the range of scores of the defined population on a measure of the variable and then selecting individuals whose scores are at the extreme of the range.
   d. by random assignment of individuals to one or the other group.
Answer: c

13. (obj. 8) After a researcher has selected a group having the characteristic he wishes to study in a causal-comparative design, the next logical step is to
   a. randomly form subgroups.
   b. identify a comparable group without the selected characteristic.
   c. collect biographical data.
   d. choose the statistical analyses to be performed.
Answer: b

14. (obj. 9) The *t* distribution should be used instead of the *z* distribution when
   a. the significance of the between-sample means is calculated.
   b. the scores of the two samples are correlated.
   c. *N* is less than 30.
   d. very large samples are studied.
Answer: c

15. (obj. 9) For which of the following hypotheses is a one-tailed test of significance appropriate?
   a. Teaching method A and teaching method B will produce different student achievement gains.
   b. There is no difference in the effects of Head Start programs on the achievement gains of low-income Caucasian and African-American children.
   c. The mean IQ score of a sample is significantly different from the population mean.
   d. Children receiving a dietary supplement will show greater achievement gains than those receiving a placebo.
Answer: d

16. (obj. 9) Use of a one-tailed versus a two-tailed t test to test the significance of the difference between two sample means depends on whether
    a. there is expected overlap between the error curves of the two sample distributions.
    b. the difference is expected to be in one direction only.
    c. the size of the samples is proportional to their respective population sizes.
    d. subjects were matched or chosen randomly.
Answer: b

17. (obj. 10) The t test for correlated means should be used when
    a. the group possessing the characteristic of interest and the comparison group are randomly selected.
    b. subgroups are to be formed within the group possessing the characteristic of interest.
    c. the group possessing the characteristic of interest and the comparison group are matched on another variable.
    d. the researcher wishes to determine the magnitude of the relationship between the independent and dependent variables.
Answer: c

18. (obj. 10) In comparing the mean performance of 25 delinquents and 25 matched nondelinquents, one should use the
    a. t test for independent means.
    b. z distribution.
    c. t test for a single mean.
    d. t test for correlated means.
Answer: d

19. (obj. 10-14) Match each condition below with the test most appropriate under that condition.
    To determine whether:
    __ 1.   the sample mean differs significantly from a specified population mean.

    __ 2.   the mean achievement of a random sample of delinquents differs significantly from that of a randomly selected control group.
    __ 3.   the mean anxiety scores of high, middle, and low achievers are significantly different.
    __ 4.   high, middle, and low achievers have different high school dropout rates.
    __ 5.   the mean achievement of two groups of students matched on aptitude differs significantly.
    a.   A t test for correlated means.
    b.   A t test for a single mean.
    c.   A chi-square test.
    d.   An analysis of variance.
    e.   A t test for independent means.
Answer: 1=b, 2=e, 3=d, 4=c, 5=a

20. (obj. 11) Use of the t test for a single mean requires
    a.   a normal score distribution.
    b.   homogeneity of variance.
    c.   random selection of subjects.
    d.   knowledge of the population mean.
Answer: d

21. (obj. 11) If a researcher wishes to determine whether a sample mean differs from the population mean, the appropriate statistic is the
    a.   chi-square.
    b. t test for independent means.
    c. t test for a single mean.
    d.   analysis of covariance.
Answer: c

141

22. (obj. 12) The F ratio is computed to determine
   a. whether the members of a sample have been randomly selected from a population.
   b. the statistical significance of the difference between the mean scores of two or more groups.
   c. whether two or more groups have different frequency distributions on a categorical variable.
   d. all of the above.
Answer: b

23. (obj. 12) Analysis of covariance is the preferred test rather than analysis of variance when
   a. initial differences between the samples on a variable related to the dependent variable need to be controlled.
   b. there are extreme differences in the sample variances.
   c. the scores of the groups being compared are in the form of categorical frequency counts.
   d. the scores of the groups being compared are in the form of ranks.
Answer: a

24. (obj. 12) In conducting a MANOVA on a cluster of five related variables, a researcher obtains an F value that is significant at the .01 level. What is the next step that should be taken in analyzing the data?
   a. Reexamine the cluster to see if any variables should be removed.
   b. Test for the equality of group dispersions.
   c. Compute a mean vector score for each variable.
   d. Compute an ANOVA on each dependent variable in the cluster.
Answer: d

25. (obj. 12) The test for homogeneity of independent variances, the test for homogeneity of related variances, and the F maximum test for homogeneity of variance are all forms of
   a. analysis of covariance.
   b. nonparametric statistics.
   c. analysis of variance.
   d. multivariate analysis of variance.
Answer: c

26. (obj. 13) A nonparametric test of significance should be considered whenever
    a. the population scores are normally distributed.
    b. group variances are equal or nearly so.
    c. scores are in the form of ranks.
    d. scores are derived from a measure with equal intervals.
Answer: c

27. (obj. 13) When research data are not normally distributed or homogeneous in variance but are in the form of interval scores, it is advisable to
    a. use parametric statistics to analyze the data.
    b. use nonparametric statistics to analyze the data.
    c. use chi-square to analyze the data.
    d. convert the scores to standard scores before analyzing the data.
Answer: a

28. (obj. 14) Chi-square should be used when data are in the form of
    a. ranks.
    b. standard scores.
    c. continuous scores.
    d. category frequencies.
Answer: d

29. (obj. 14) The Mann-Whitney U test, the Wilcoxon signed rank test, and the Kruskal-Wallis test
    a. all are forms of chi-square.
    b. are preferred when the research data are rank or interval scores that grossly violate parametric assumptions of normal distribution and homogeneity of variance.
    c. are used to compare the score distributions of three or more groups.
    d. all of the above.
Answer: b

OPEN-FORM ITEMS

1. (obj. 1) Briefly describe the different role of description in descriptive research and in causal-comparative research.
Answer:
In descriptive research, the role of description is simply to describe phenomena as they are. In causal-comparative research, the purpose is to describe phenomena as they relate to other phenomena and to infer possible cause-effect relationships among those phenomena.

2. (obj. 2) Name two descriptive statistics that often are calculated in a descriptive research study.
Answer (any 2 OK):
    a. The mean.
    b. The median.
    c. The mode.
    d. The standard deviation.
    e. The variance.
    f. The range.

3. (obj. 3) A researcher makes direct observations of the classroom question-asking behavior of third graders. What type of descriptive research does this study exemplify?
Answer:
The research involves description of a sample at one point in time.

4. (obj. 4) In longitudinal research, describe how samples are selected for (a) cohort, (b) trend and (c) panel studies, and provide an example of each sampling procedure.
Answer:
    a. In *trend* studies a random sample from a general population whose members change over time (e.g., all members of the American Federation of Teachers) is selected at each data-collection point. Thus, both the population and the sample are different at each data collection point.
    b. In *cohort* studies a random sample of a fixed population whose members stay the same (e.g., the 1988 graduating class from Hoover High School) is selected at each data collection point. Thus the population remains the same, but the sample is different at each data-collection point.
    c. In *panel* studies, a sample is selected at the start of the study, and the same sample is surveyed at each data-collection point (e.g., a group of Hoover High School students who agree at the time of graduation to provide data to the researcher every 10 years). Thus both the population and the sample remains the same at each data collection point.

5. (obj. 4) Lewis Terman's study of giftedness involved repeated measurement of a panel of children identified as geniuses at various stages in their lives. What is one weakness and one strength of this study design?
Answer (any 1 from each set OK):
Weaknesses
a. Having been given the instrument or interview before can affect individuals' responses at the next data collection point.
b. The response rate tends to decline with repeated follow-ups.
c. Loss of subjects can reduce the representativeness of the sample.
Strengths
a. Because the same individuals are measured at each data-collection point, the panel design is sensitive to smaller changes than comparably sized samples in cohort or trend studies.
b. Because the same individuals are measured at each data-collection point, the researcher can trace the specific past experiences and characteristics of individuals that might have contributed to changes observed over time.

6. (obj. 5) Describe the major problem with the sampling procedure used in a cross-sectional research design, and provide an example that illustrates that problem.
Answer:
Over time the population that is sampled is likely to change through attrition. Thus the sample that is selected to represent the population at one stage of development may not be representative of the population at other stages of development. For example, comparing the incidence of smoking among teens, young adults, and older adults through a cross-sectional design might involve a biased sample of older adults, because some individuals who have smoked from an early age may have become ill or died by the time they would reach this age and thus are not part of the accessible population.

7. (obj. 6) A researcher finds a correlation between length of teaching experience (variable X) and the principal's ratings of teaching effectiveness (variable Y) for the teachers employed in the principal's school. Give two plausible interpretations of this finding.
Answer (any 2 OK):
a.   As teachers gain more experience, they become more effective, i.e., X leads to Y.
b.   The more effective teachers are more likely to survive staffing cuts and also to choose to continue teaching, i.e., Y leads to X.
c.   Both teacher longevity (X) and rated teaching effectiveness (Y) are a function of some other variable, e.g., teachers' emotional stability (Z), i.e., Z leads to both X and Y.

8. (objs. 7-8) Describe two approaches to selecting a suitable comparison group for a causal-comparative research study.
Answer:

   a. Draw two groups from the same population, measure whether the two groups differ on any extraneous variables that could affect the study results, and if so, match the groups on those variables.

   b. Select comparison groups who are at the two extremes of the distribution on one of the variables of interest but who are similar in other respects.

9. (obj. 9) List three assumptions about the obtained scores in a causal-comparative study that should be satisfied in order to use the *t* test.
Answer:
   a. The scores form an interval or ratio scale of measurement.
   b. Scores in the defined populations are normally distributed.
   c. Score variances for the defined populations are equal.

10. (obj. 10) Under what condition should the researcher use the *t* test for correlated means in a causal-comparative study, and what effect will use of this type of *t* test have on the likelihood of finding a significant difference between groups on the variable of interest?
Answer:
The *t* test for correlated means is appropriate when the researcher has matched the groups to be compared on an extraneous variable that is correlated with the dependent variable. Under this condition, the *t* test for correlated means is more likely to yield a statistically significant difference than a *t* test for independent means.

11. (obj. 11) A researcher wishes to determine whether the sample's mean score on a standardized achievement test is different from the mean score of the norming group. What type of *t* test is most appropriate in this situation?
Answer: The *t* test for a single mean is most appropriate, because the researcher is comparing the sample's mean score to that of the presumed mean score of the population, as estimated by the norming group's mean score.

12. (obj. 12) A researcher conducts a study in which 90 high school sophomores are randomly assigned to three algebra classes. Class A is taught by a lecture method, class B by a cooperative learning method, and class C by an individualized method. Algebra achievement, the dependent variable, is measured at the end of the course. What statistical significance test is most appropriate for comparing the mean algebra achievement scores of the three groups? If this test yields a value that is significant at the .05 level, how would you interpret this finding?
Answer:
Analysis of variance would be the appropriate statistical test. An F ratio that is significant at the .05 level indicates that a significant difference exists between at least one pair of the mean scores, but it does not indicate which pair were significantly different.

13. (obj. 12) What is the major difference between analysis of variance (ANOVA) and analysis of covariance (ANCOVA)?
Answer:
ANCOVA adjusts statistically for initial group differences on one or more variables (called covariates).

14. (obj. 13) Three assumptions about population parameters should be checked when deciding to use parametric statistics to analyze causal-comparative data rather than nonparametric statistics. List one of these assumptions.
Answer (any 1 OK):
    a.   The scores in the population are normally distributed on the variables being studied.
    b.   The population variances of the comparison groups are approximately equal.
    c.   The scores being analyzed are derived from a measure that has equal intervals.

15. (obj. 14) You have hypothesized that dogmatism is distributed among army recruits so as to approximate a normal distribution (or normal probability curve). You randomly select 1,000 recruits at a basic training center and administer the Rokeach Dogmatism Scale. Scores of the 1,000 subjects are sorted into five categories ranging from high dogmatism to low dogmatism. What statistical procedure would be most appropriate to test your hypothesis, and why?
Answer:
Chi-square is the most appropriate test, because you have categorical data that you want to check against a normal distribution.

APPLICATION PROBLEMS

Problem 1
Two researchers are interested in doing a study to provide descriptive information to a school district about homelessness among students attending the district's schools. One researcher is a quantitative researcher, and the other is a qualitative researcher. Assume that they are able to obtain information from school records about all the students who are categorized as homeless. Describe (a) several types of information that the quantitative researcher would be more likely to report, and (b) several types of information that the qualitative researcher would be more likely to report.
Sample Answer:

a. The quantitative researcher probably would want to report the number and proportion of students in the district who are homeless, and, perhaps, the average length of time that students have been homeless. She might be interested in classifying students by their current types of living arrangements (e.g., living in an established shelter for homeless people; living in a vehicle, tent, or other constructed personal dwelling; or not living in any permanent arrangement but being on the move); she might then calculate the percentage of homeless students in each category.

b. The qualitative researcher probably would want to report in-depth information from a purposeful sample of homeless students who are willing to be interviewed. She might explore such topics as their feelings about being homeless and the particular challenges it presents to them in relation to attending school and doing schoolwork.

Problem 2
Describe a suitable comparison group for each of the following defined groups in a causal-comparative study.

a. The discipline styles used by parents of high school students with high scores on an authoritarianism scale.

b. The extent to which female college students who are in leadership roles in campus organizations report childhood experiences in which adults encouraged them to display leadership.

c. The educational aspirations of fourth-grade Pueblo Indian boys who have attended school only on the reservation.
Sample Answer:

a. Parents of high school students who have low scores on the authoritarianism scale.

b. Female college students who are not in leadership roles in campus organizations.

c. Fourth-grade Pueblo Indian boys who have attended school off the reservation.

Problem 3

A researcher studies the difference in reading achievement of third-grade children who learned to read by the phonics method and those who learned to read by the whole language method of teaching reading. Children in the two groups are matched on scholastic aptitude. What type of t test should the investigator use to analyze the results, and why? If the t value is significant, what interpretation can the researcher make?

Sample Answer:

The t test for correlated means is appropriate because children were matched for scholastic aptitude, which probably is correlated with the dependent variable, reading achievement. A significant t means either that students taught by the phonics method showed superior reading achievement or that students taught by the whole-language method showed superior reading achievement; this can be determined by examining the mean reading achievement scores of each group. The researcher needs to be cautious, however, in claiming that the teaching method caused the higher level of reading achievement. Even though the groups were matched on aptitude, another variable might be responsible for the differences in post-treatment reading achievement, e.g. motivation.

Problem 4

You hypothesize that low-achieving children who receive special tutoring will make significantly greater reading achievement gains than those who spend an equal amount of time engaged in solitary reading in the regular classroom. Would this hypothesis be tested with a one-tailed or a two-tailed test of significance, and why?

Sample Answer:

A one-tailed test is appropriate because you have predicted the direction of the difference that is expected between the gains of the two groups. Also, you can refer to previous research showing a relationship between tutoring and increased scholastic achievement. Thus, if a difference is found, it probably will favor the group that received special tutoring.

Problem 5

A researcher is interested in learning whether attendance at a high school with strict rules of discipline and conduct tends to produce authoritarian students. He locates two high schools that are located in very similar neighborhoods serving similar racial and socioeconomic groups. School A promotes strict rules of discipline and conduct, and most of its teachers and administrators have higher than average scores on a measure of authoritarianism. School B employs flexible rules of discipline and conduct, has a high level of student involvement in formulating school rules, and primarily employs teachers and administrators with lower than average scores on a test of authoritarianism.

a. In a pilot study the researcher randomly selects 25 students from each school and administers a 40-item scale of authoritarianism. What statistical technique should be used to analyze these data?

b. Each high school has 12 extracurricular programs that are classified by a group of independent judges as either high, average, or low in terms of authoritarian structure and activities. The researcher wishes to compare the proportion of students in each school who participated in each of the three types of programs. What statistical technique should be used to make this comparison?

c. In checking school records, the researcher found that most seniors in the two high schools had been administered the California F scale (a measure of authoritarianism) during their last year of junior high school. He decides to administer a different but similar authoritarianism measure to seniors who had taken the earlier test, and then see how the senior-level authoritarianism scores differed between students in the two schools when their earlier scores were taken into consideration. What statistical technique should be used?

Sample Answer:

a. A *t* test for uncorrelated means would be used to compare the authoritarianism scores of the two samples.

b. A chi-square test would be conducted on the percentage of students in each cell of the following table:

	High Authoritarianism	Average Authoritarianism	Low Authoritarianism
School A			
School B			

c. Analysis of covariance should be used, because it permits adjusting the senior high school authoritarianism scores for differences found in the junior high school authoritarianism scores.

TEACHING ACTIVITIES

Activity 1
Have students read an educational research study that involved describing the characteristics of a sample at one point in time. (The study by Glesne and Webb discussed in chapter 6 of the text, involving a questionnaire survey, is an example.) Ask the students to write a brief paper in which they specify how a longitudinal study could be carried out with the same target population, measures, and procedures. Tell students to be sure to specify whether the longitudinal research design would involve a trend study, a cohort study, or a panel study, and why they chose that study design.

Activity 2
Identify a research report that describes a causal-comparative study involving two groups, and have students read it as a homework assignment. Discuss in class the following features of the study: statement of the research problem, selection of the defined group and the comparison group, the measures and procedures used to measure the dependent variable, the statistical test used to test the difference between the means of the two groups, and the findings.

Activity 3
Have each student make up a research problem for which chi-square would be the appropriate statistical test. Tell them to specify the purpose of the study, the variables to be measured, and the sampling procedure. You also can do this activity with other statistical tests described in chapter 10, e.g., analysis of variance and analysis of covariance.

CHAPTER 11
CORRELATIONAL RESEARCH DESIGNS

Note: The phrase in parentheses following the item number for both closed-form and open-form items, for example, 1. (obj. 3), refers to the textbook chapter objective to which the item is keyed.

CLOSED-FORM ITEMS

1. (obj. 1) An advantage of the correlational method is that
   a. it can be used to analyze the relationships among many variables within a single study.
   b. it indicates both the direction and the degree of the relationship between variables.
   c. it can be used to predict academic achievement and other outcomes.
   d. all of the above.

Answer: d

2. (obj. 2) A scattergram provides a visual representation of
   a. the causal relationship between two measured variables.
   b. the standard error of measurement for two measured variables.
   c. whether the relationship between two measured variables is positive or negative.
   d. the results of a path analysis.

Answer: c

3. (obj. 2) If every point in a scattergram plotting variable X and variable Y falls on the line of best fit, we can conclude that
   a. variable X predicts measured variable Y perfectly.
   b. variable X explains none of the variance in variable y.
   c. the relationship between variables X and Y is positive.
   d. the relationship between variables X and Y is negative.

Answer: a

4. (obj. 3) If every increase in score on a test of literary knowledge is accompanied by an increase in score on an intelligence test, one can conclude that
   a. there is a perfect positive relationship between literary knowledge and intelligence.
   b. there is a perfect negative relationship between literary knowledge and intelligence.
   c. the correlation between the literary knowledge and intelligence tests is .00.
   d. the correlation between the literary knowledge and intelligence tests is .50.
Answer: a

5. (obj. 3) A researcher who obtains a correlation of -.72 between test anxiety and college gradepoint average would be justified in concluding that
   a. scores on the two variables do not covary substantially.
   b. students who experience a great deal of test anxiety have a tendency to get lower grades than students who experience minimal test anxiety.
   c. low test anxiety inhibits college achievement.
   d. high test anxiety is associated with higher grades.
Answer: b

6. (obj. 4) The purpose of a relationship study typically is to
   a. determine whether the relationship between two measured variables is caused by overlapping items.
   b. identify possible causes or effects of observed phenomena.
   c. check how well two observers agree in their ratings of the same phenomena.
   d. check how well the scores on individual items of a test relate to each other.
Answer: b

7. (obj. 4) A limitation of the shotgun approach to identify variables that correlate with a criterion variable is that
   a. it cannot detect whether the observed relationships are positive or negative.
   b. it cannot detect the magnitude of the observed relationships.
   c. only a few variables can be accommodated in the research design.
   d. some of the many measured variables are likely to correlate with the criterion by chance.
Answer: d

8. (obj. 4) In research investigating relationships between variables, it is best if
   a. the research sample is homogeneous with respect to major demographic variables.
   b. the number of variables is approximately the same as the number of individuals in the sample.
   c. the researcher uses the individual as the unit of statistical analysis.
   d. the researcher uses the group as the unit of statistical analysis.

Answer: a

9. (obj. 5) In a prediction study, the basic form of data analysis consists of
   a. analysis of covariance.
   b. comparing the variances of different predictor variables.
   c. correlating each moderator variable with the criterion variable.
   d. correlating each predictor variable with the criterion variable.

Answer: d

10. (obj. 5) Both multiple regression and moderator analysis can be used to
   a. determine underlying factors in a set of variables.
   b. check for item overlap as a cause of an observed correlation between two measured variables.
   c. maximize the correlation between predictor variables and a criterion.
   d. control for shrinkage in predictive validity coefficients.

Answer: c

11. (obj. 6) Prediction research can be done for the purpose of
   a. studying the validity of a new aptitude test.
   b. determining which individuals are most likely to benefit from a residential treatment program.
   c. testing a theory about the determinants of administrative effectiveness.
   d. all of the above.

Answer: d

12. (obj. 7) The effectiveness of a measure in identifying which individuals will be successful with respect to a given criterion depends upon its predictive validity, the selection ratio, and the
   a. amount of variance accounted for by the correlation coefficient.
   b. proportion of individuals who would be successful if no selection procedure was used.
   c. size of the sample.
   d. direction of the validity coefficient.

Answer: b

13. (obj. 7) Cross-validation of findings from a prediction study is particularly important for
    a. determining the stability of the base rate.
    b. improving the selection ratio.
    c. identifying nonlinear relationships between variables.
    d. checking for shrinkage.
Answer: d

14. (obj. 8) An important factor in deciding which correlational technique to use is
    a. the form in which the data are expressed.
    b. the sample size.
    c. the type of cause-effect relationship being studied.
    d. whether the relationship is hypothesized to be positive or negative.
Answer: a

15. (obj. 8) An important reason for making a scattergram is that it
    a. provides a test of the statistical significance of the obtained correlation coefficient.
    b. provides a measure of the confidence limits for the obtained correlation coefficient.
    c. is helpful for detecting nonlinear relationships.
    d. provides an estimate of the amount of shrinkage in a correlation coefficient when cross-validated.
Answer: c

16. (obj. 9) The correction for attenuation estimates what the magnitude of the correlation between two measured variables would be if
    a. a cross-validation study was done.
    b. the measures were perfectly reliable.
    c. the raw scores were converted to standard scores.
    d. the influence of moderator variables was partialled out.
Answer: b

17. (obj. 9) To correct for restriction in range, the researcher must know the
    a. true correlation between the measured variables in the population.
    b. size of the population.
    c. reliability of each measured variable.
    d. variability of population scores.
Answer: d

18. (obj. 9) To hold intelligence constant when correlating scores on a Spanish achievement test and a measure of auditory acuity, a researcher should use
    a. partial correlation.
    b. correction for attenuation.
    c. the correlation ratio.
    d. factor analysis.
Answer: a

19. (obj. 10) Multiple regression involves
    a. generating a correlation matrix.
    b. determining the correlation between a criterion variable and a combination of predictor variables.
    c. testing for cause-and-effect relationships along a path of variables.
    d. identifying measured variables that correlate with each other, but not with other variables in a data set.
Answer: b

20. (obj. 10) A researcher administers 10 measures of stress and anxiety to a sample of evaluators working for state departments of education. What statistical technique can the researcher use to determine whether the information in these 10 measures can be reduced to a smaller number of variables?
    a. Factor analysis.
    b. Multiple regression analysis.
    c. Path analysis.
    d. Discriminant analysis.
Answer: a

21. (obj. 10) The multiple correlation coefficient between five predictor variables and grades is .50. This finding means that
    a. the best single predictor explains 25 percent of the variance in grades.
    b. the average correlation between each predictor variable and grades is .10.
    c. the combined set of predictor variables explains 25 percent of the variance in grades.
    d. the combined predictor battery explains 50 percent of the variance in grades.
Answer: c

22. (obj. 10) If a researcher wishes to determine how well a combination of predictor variables correlates with a composite of several criterion variables, the appropriate statistical technique to use is
    a. path analysis.
    b. discriminant analysis.
    c. structural equation modeling.
    d. canonical correlation.
Answer: d

23. (obj. 10) Path analysis is an appropriate statistical technique when
    a. the criterion variable is a dichotomy.
    b. the criterion is a composite of variables.
    c. the researcher wishes to test a theory about the causal relationships among a set of variables.
    d. the researcher wishes to identify clusters of related variables.
Answer: c

24. (obj. 10) An advantage of structural equation modeling over path analysis is that it
    a. is much simpler to compute.
    b. requires fewer measured variables.
    c. yields more valid and reliable measures of the variables to be analyzed.
    d. can be used when some or all of the variables are measured as dichotomies or ranks.
Answer: c

25. (obj. 11) Suppose a researcher generates a correlation matrix for four variables. How many correlation coefficients would be in the matrix?
    a. 9.
    b. 6.
    c. 4.
    d. 10.
Answer: b

26. (obj. 11) A correlation matrix is used to
    a. show the extent to which each variable in a set of variables correlates with all the other variables in the set.
    b. determine which predictor variables to enter into a multiple regression equation.
    c. identify variables that have a restricted range.
    d. all of the above.
Answer: a

27. (obj. 12) Aptitude test scores generally predict school grades better for females than for males. This finding indicates that
    a. aptitude is a moderator variable.
    b. gender is a predictor variable.
    c. gender is a moderator variable.
    d. a correction for attenuation is needed.
Answer: c

28. (obj. 13) The size of a research sample
    a. determines the type of correlation coefficient that should be calculated.
    b. affects the magnitude of an obtained correlation coefficient.
    c. has a minor effect on the statistical significance of a correlation coefficient.
    d. has a large effect on the statistical significance of a correlation coefficient.
Answer: d

29. (obj. 13) A correlation coefficient of .20 between two variables
    a. is too small to have practical significance for education.
    b. is sufficiently large to have practical significance for education.
    c. is sufficiently large to have practical significance for education, but only if the measured variables are linked to a proven theory.
    d. is sufficiently large to have practical significance in education, but not in medicine.
Answer: b

CLOSED-FORM ITEMS

1. (obj. 1) State one advantage and one limitation of correlational research.
Answer:
   Advantages
   a.   The relationships among a large number of variables can be investigated in a single study.
   b.   It enables the study of possible causal relationships among certain phenomena that cannot be experimentally manipulated.
   c.   It provides information on both the degree and the direction of the relationship between the variables being studied.
   Limitations
   a.   Cause-and-effect relationships cannot be established with a high level of certainty.
   b.   Correlational studies of a complex behavior pattern or characteristic sometimes focus on atomistic variables that do not accurately reflect the pattern or characteristic. As a result, the studies yield data that are difficult or impossible to interpret.

2. (obj. 2) Describe two types of information that can be obtained from examination of a scattergram of a group's scores on two variables.
Answer (any 2 OK):
   a.   The direction of the relationship between the two variables.
   b.   The degree of the relationship between the two variables.
   c.   Whether the relationship between the two variables is linear or nonlinear.

3. (obj. 3) The correlation between variable X and variable Y is .40. What does this correlation coefficient tell us about: (a) the explained variance in the relationship between X and Y,(b) the direction of the relationship, and (c) whether the relationship is causal?
Answer:
   a.   Variable X explains 16 percent of the variance in variable Y.
   b.   The direction of the relationship is positive, meaning that higher scores on variable X tend to be associated with higher scores on variable Y.
   c.   The obtained correlation coefficient is consistent with a presumed causal relationship between variables X and Y, but does not prove that such a relationship exists.

4. (obj. 4) Suppose that you are interested in the nature of ability in graphic art. You identify several variables that you hypothesize to have a causal relationship to artistic ability, such as depth perception, hand-eye coordination, creative imagination and so on.

    a.   What type of correlational study would you do with these variables to explore the causes of ability in graphic art?

    b.   How would this study be conducted?

Answer:

    a.   A relationship study.

    b.   In a simple relationship study the artistic ability of a group of individuals would be quantified (e.g., artistic work could be rated). A measure of each of the possible causal variables also would be obtained. Correlations would be computed between the criterion and each causal variable.

5. (obj. 5) A researcher has two sets of scores for a sample of graduating seniors: their scores on a vocabulary test administered just before graduation, and their cumulative gradepoint average (GPA). The researcher finds a high positive correlation between the two sets of scores, and therefore recommends that the vocabulary test be administered to high school freshmen to identify those who are likely to experience academic difficulty during high school. What is the major flaw in this recommendation?

Answer:

The measure of the predictor variable (i.e., the vocabulary test) was administered at the same time as the measure of the criterion variable (i.e., cumulative GPA). The predictive validity of the vocabulary test needs to be established by administering it to students during their freshmen year and then determining their cumulative GPA four years later.

6. (obj. 6) Briefly describe two uses of prediction research.

Answer (any 2 OK):

    a.   Prediction studies can determine the extent to which some criterion behavior can be predicted. Such studies, if successful, often lead to the development of selection systems such as those employed in college, industry, and the military.

    b.   Prediction studies can be used in theory building. A theory can be tested by making predictions based upon the theory and then doing prediction studies to see if the theory holds up.

    c.   Prediction studies are employed to establish the predictive validity of tests, which can subsequently be employed in practical problems of selection and prediction.

7. (obj. 7) A researcher conducts a study of gifted children to determine which of 50 predictor variables are related to academic achievement in a summer enrichment program. They find that three of the measured variables are good predictors. Why is it important to replicate this study before using these predictor variables in selecting students for the program?

Answer:

Because so many predictor variables were measured, it is likely that some correlated significantly with the criterion by chance. To determine whether this is true, it is necessary to cross-validate the significant predictors with another sample. If the original results occurred by chance, the correlation coefficients for the significant predictor variables are likely to "shrink" in the cross-validation study.

8. (obj. 8)
    a.   Under what condition would a researcher be likely to compute a correlation ratio?
    b.   Why is this type of correlation coefficient superior to other types under this condition?

Answer:

    a.   The correlation ratio is computed when there is reason to believe that the relationship between two variables is nonlinear.

    b.   The correlation ratio yields a more accurate measure of the magnitude of a nonlinear relationship between two variables than other types of correlation coefficients. The other types will underestimate the magnitude of the relationship.

9. (obj. 9) You are interested in the relationship between anxiety and the willingness to take risks among cadets in training to become police officers. You select a random sample of 200 police officers in a large city and administer a standard anxiety scale with a reliability of .82 and a risk-taking test with a reliability of .68. The correlation you obtain is .42.

    a.   What technique would you use to estimate what the correlation between anxiety and risk-taking would be if you had perfectly reliable measures?

    b.   You believe that the sample in your study is much less variable in anxiety than the national population of police officers, having very few cases with low anxiety scores. What technique would you use to estimate what the correlation between anxiety and risk-taking would be if your sample had been as variable as the national population?

Answer:

    a.   Correction for attenuation.

    b.   Correction for restriction in range.

10. (obj. 10) A researcher is investigating the factors that underlie success or failure in high school mathematics. She measures 30 predictor variables and five criterion variables relating to mathematics learning (e.g., gradepoint average in mathematics coursework, attitudes toward mathematics, and number of mathematics courses taken). What correlation technique should be used to determine (a) which combination of predictor variables best predicts mathematics gradepoint average, (b) which combination of predictor variables best predicts whether a student takes or does not take a course on calculus (which is a dichotomous variable), (c) whether the data support a theoretical model linking some of the predictor variables to one of the criterion variables, and (d) whether there are commonalities in the 30 predictor variables such that they can be reduced to a smaller number of underlying variables?
Answer:
    a.   Multiple regression.
    b.   Discriminant analysis.
    c.   Path analysis or structural equation modeling.
    d.   Factor analysis.

11. (obj. 11) What is the purpose of a correlation matrix?
Answer:
The correlation matrix provides a visual display of the correlation coefficient for every pair of variables in a research study. By examining the correlation matrix, the researcher can determine how well a particular variable correlates with all the other variables.

12. (obj. 12) A researcher obtains a correlation coefficient of .29 between scores on a diagnostic test and a test of first-grade reading achievement for a large sample of ethnically diverse children.
    a.   Why might the researcher do a follow-up correlational analysis in which this correlation coefficient is computed separately for the major ethnic groups in the sample?
    b.   What is the technical term for the variable of ethnicity in the follow-up analysis?
Answer:
    a.   The correlation coefficient of .29 for the total sample might be higher or lower for particular ethnic subgroups.
    b.   Ethnicity is a moderator variable in this analysis.

13. (obj. 13) What are two factors that determine whether an obtained correlation coefficient will be statistically significant?
Answer (any 2 OK):
    a.   The magnitude of the correlation coefficient.
    b.   The sample size.
    c.   Whether a one-tailed or two-tailed test of statistical significance is done.

APPLICATION PROBLEMS

1. A researcher intercorrelates a number of measures she has collected on a sample of college seniors. She finds a correlation of .65 between (1) the amount of time a student has been employed during his or her college years and (2) a paper-and-pencil measure of the student's personal maturity. On the basis of this finding, would she justified in concluding that

    a.   the college should institute a work-study program in order to increase the maturity level of its students? Explain your answer.

    b.   the longer students have worked during college, the higher will be their score on the personal maturity measure? Explain your answer.

    c.   more mature students are better able to obtain jobs while in college than their less mature peers? Explain your answer.

Sample Answer:

    a.   No. This conclusion assumes that there is a causal connection between working while in college and degree of personal maturity. Causal inferences cannot be made with a high degree of assurance from correlational data.

    b.   Yes. The correlation of .65 means that the two variables are positively related, that is, an increment in the amount of employment is likely to be associated with an increment in personal maturity score.

    c.   No. As in (a) above, this conclusion makes a causal assumption that is not warranted on the basis of the correlational data obtained in this study.

Problem 2

A researcher decides to investigate possible determinants of interest in science among elementary school children. First he develops and validates a measure of this variable. Then he locates tests that measure as many variables as possible in as short a time as possible to correlate with his interest test. His reasoning is that he will increase the likelihood of discovering significant relationships if he maximizes the number of variables in the correlational design. What is wrong with the researcher's reasoning?

Sample Answer:

Increasing the number of variables (an example of the shotgun approach) will not necessarily increase the likelihood of finding significant relationships. Also, some of the variables may correlate significantly with the criterion variables for irrelevant reasons. These correlations probably will disappear when the study's findings are cross-validated. A better strategy is to measure variables that theory and previous research findings suggest are related to the criterion variable (i.e., interest in science).

3. A researcher has collected a large amount of data on a sample of college students: scores on the Stanford-Binet Intelligence Scale, scores on the Wechsler Adult Intelligence Scale, scores on the Scholastic Aptitude Test (SAT), high school class rank, scores on a test anxiety scale, and whether the students successfully completed the first year of college (pass-fail and gradepoint average). Answer the following questions about the appropriate correlational analyses to be conducted on these data:

    a.   What correlational technique should be used to determine whether scores on the Stanford-Binet are related to scores on the Wechsler scale? Why this technique?

    b.   The researcher finds that test anxiety correlates significantly with the criterion variable of gradepoint average in the first year of college. The SAT also correlates significantly with test anxiety and the criterion. What statistical technique should be used to determine the correlation between test anxiety and college gradepoint average after the influence of SAT on both variables has been removed?

    c.   What correlational technique should be used to determine whether all of the tests used in this study, when intercorrelated, measure a common factor?

    d.   What correlational technique should be used to determine whether the relationship between scores on the test anxiety scale and high school class rank is nonlinear?

Sample Answer:

    a.   Product-moment correlation coefficient, because both scales yield continuous scores.

    b.   Partial correlation, because this statistical technique is used to determine the degree of relationship between two variables after the effect of a third variable on both has been removed.

    c.   Factor analysis, because this technique determines the extent to which all the measures entered into a correlation matrix represent the same basic behavior pattern or characteristic.

    d.   The correlation ratio *eta*. It may be helpful to first prepare a scattergram of the data to check for nonlinearity in the relationship between the two sets of scores.

Problem 4

A researcher administered a battery of 20 different tests to a group of entering medical students. She also collected their gradepoint average (GPA) at the end of their first year of medical school. What statistical technique should be used to maximize the usefulness of the 20 tests as predictors of GPA, and why?

Sample Answer:

Multiple regression, because this statistical technique yields a better prediction than could be obtained by correlating any single test with the criterion variable, that is, GPA.

Problem 5

A researcher administered a personality inventory that measures 15 personality traits to a group of entering students in a doctoral program in education. He also determined their gradepoint average (GPA) at the end of the first year of the program. He then used multiple regression to determine which combination of personality traits best predicts GPA in this situation. The following is his table of results.

Personality Variable	Beta	Correlation Coefficient (r)	Multiple Correlation (R)	R^2	R^2 Increment
Conformity	.35	.28	.28	.08	
Independence	.26	.15	.34	.12	.04
Introversion	.21	.11	.37	.14	.02

    a. What information is provided by the beta weights in the first data column?

    b. What information is provided by the fact that the beta weight for conformity is .35, whereas for introversion it is .21?

    c. What does the correlation coefficient of .15 for independence in the second data column mean?

    d. What does the multiple correlation coefficient of .37 in the third data column mean?

    e. What does the R^2 value of .08 in the fourth data column mean?

    f. What does the R^2 increment of .02 in the fifth data column mean?

Sample Answer:

    a. The beta weights indicate the predictive value of each personality variable in the multiple regression equation.

    b. The difference in these beta weights indicates that the personality variable of conformity has more predictive value than introversion in the multiple regression equation.

    c. It indicates that the measure of independence correlates .15 with GPA, meaning that there is a slight tendency for higher scores on the independence measure to be associated with a higher GPA.

    d. It means that the combination of the measures of conformity, independence, and introversion correlate .37 with GPA.

    e. It means that the measure of conformity explains 8 percent of the variance in the students' GPA.

    f. It means that adding the measure of introversion to the multiple regression equation explains another two percent of the variance in the students' GPA.

Problem 6

Researcher A correlates scores on a predictor variable and a criterion variable and obtains a correlation coefficient that is statistically significant but of no practical significance. Researcher B correlates scores on a different predictor variable and the same criterion variable and obtains a correlation coefficient that is not statistically significant but of practical significance.

   a.   How can researcher B's correlation coefficient be significant in a practical sense but not in a statistical sense?

   b.   How can researcher A's correlation coefficient be significant in a statistical sense but not in a practical sense?

Sample Answer:

   a.   Practical significance depends primarily on the magnitude of the obtained correlation coefficient. Thus, researcher B's obtained correlation coefficient must have been larger than researcher A's obtained correlation coefficient.

   b.   Statistical significance depends not only on the magnitude of the correlation coefficient but also on the sample size. If researcher A's sample size was much larger than that of researcher B, this would explain why researcher A's obtained correlation coefficient was statistically significant even though its magnitude was smaller.

Problem 7

(Note: This is a complex problem that might be assigned as a long homework assignment. It requires a data bank and access to a statistical package on a computer or calculator.)

   a.   Study the data bank provided by your instructor.

   b.   Select any two variables that you want to study. These variables can be in any score form (e.g., continuous scores or ranks). List the two variables and their score form.

   c.   Select the group(s) in the data bank from which you will draw your sample. If you will sample from the group(s) rather than studying the entire group(s), describe your sampling procedure.

   d.   Write the null hypothesis that you will test in your study, and the alpha level you will use for rejecting the null hypothesis.

   e.   List all the members of the sample and their scores on the two variables to be correlated.

   f.   State the correlational technique that you will use to analyze your data, and explain why you chose this technique.

   g.   Describe the procedures that you followed in using a calculator or computer to determine the correlation between the two variables.

   h.   Prepare a statement of your results and a brief discussion of their meaning and limitations.

166

TEACHING ACTIVITIES

Activity 1
Identify a research article that describes a relationship study or a prediction study employing correlational statistics. (Several prediction studies are listed in chapter 11 of the textbook.) Have all students read the study as a homework assignment and then discuss in class the technical aspects of the study's research methodology and the study's strengths and weaknesses. This activity also can be repeated with published research studies that highlight the use of other correlational techniques, e.g., multiple regression, factor analysis, and path analysis.

Activity 2
If students have no prior experience with statistics, you can have them collect data on two variables that you are confident are correlated with each other, for example, the height and weight of people whom they know. You can prepare a transparency that contains a graph on which such data can be plotted. The students can bring their data to class, and you can show them how the data are plotted on the graph to produce a scattergram. You can use the scattergram to show students the line of best fit for the data and to discuss the concept of explained variance.

Activity 3
Multiple regression is an important correlational technique that may be unfamiliar to students, even if they have taken a statistics course. You can find a multiple regression equation in a published research study (or use the example in the textbook) and explain how it works in class.

This activity also can be done with factor analysis, another important correlational technique often not covered in elementary statistics courses. You can show students the various outputs of a factor analysis (e.g., correlation matrix, factors, and factor loadings) and explain what they mean.

CHAPTER 12
EXPERIMENTAL DESIGNS, PART 1

Note: The phrase in parentheses following the item number for both closed-form and open-form items, for example, 1. (obj. 3), refers to the textbook chapter objective to which the item is keyed.

CLOSED-FORM ITEMS

1. (obj. 1) Match each type of extraneous variable below with the appropriate example.
   __ 1.   A pretest similar to the posttest is administered before the experimental treatment.
   __ 2.   Students below the 15th percentile in reading achievement who volunteer are placed in the experimental group, and nonvolunteers at the same reading level are placed in the control group.
   __ 3.   During the experiment students are exposed to a variety of special instructional experiences that are not part of the experimental treatment.
   __ 4.   Low achievers drop out at a higher rate than other students from an individualized reading program designed to improve reading achievement.
   __ 5.   A group of students who fall below the 15th percentile on a reading achievement test earns higher scores on the posttest following an experimental treatment, whereas a group of students who fall above the 85th percentile earns lower scores on the same posttest following the same experimental treatment.
   __ 6.   Students who attend summer camp three years in a row show annual increases on a measure of physical strength.
      a.   History.
      b.   Maturation.
      c.   Testing.
      d.   Experimental treatment diffusion.
      e.   Statistical regression.
      f.   Differential selection.
      g.   Experimental mortality.
   Answer: 1=c, 2=f, 3=a, 4=g, 5=e, 6=b

2. The internal validity of an experiment refers to its
   a. generalizability to a defined population.
   b. use of valid measurement instruments.
   c. control of extraneous variables.
   d. control of testing effects.
   Answer: c

3. (obj. 1) A group of teachers receives access to the Internet as part of their participation in an experiment. The school district's administrators decide that this is a good idea, and provide Internet access for all teachers in the district, including control group teachers. The administrators' action weakens internal validity through
    a.   resentful demoralization of the control group.
    b.   compensatory equalization of treatments.
    c.   compensatory rivalry by the control group.
    d.   differential selection.

Answer: b

4. (obj. 2) Multiple-treatment interference refers to the situation in which
    a.   subjects' performance on the dependent variable reflects the combined effect of more than one treatment.
    b.   extraneous variables rather than the experimental treatment are responsible for the experimental outcome.
    c.   high correlations between pretest and posttest scores reduce the chances of significant gain scores.
    d.   control-group subjects are affected by their knowledge of the experimental treatment.

Answer: a

5. (obj. 2) Students' racial attitudes are measured by a paper-and-pencil test immediately before and after viewing a film denouncing racial prejudice. What threat to the external validity of the experiment does this procedure raise?
    a.   Statistical regression.
    b.   Attribute-treatment interaction.
    c.   Multiple-treatment interference.
    d.   Pretest sensitization.

Answer: d

6. (obj. 2) In the Hawthorne effect, individuals who participate in an experiment improve their performance because
   a. they are aware that they are participating in an experiment.
   b. the experiment is a novel experience for them.
   c. they like the experimenter.
   d. the posttest is easier than the pretest.
Answer: a

7. (obj. 3) A researcher provides an extensive orientation to introduce research participants to the experimental treatment. The purpose of this orientation probably is to
   a. control for experimental treatment diffusion.
   b. control for history.
   c. strengthen the representativeness of the experimental design.
   d. control for pretest sensitization.
Answer: c

8. (obj. 3) An experiment that incorporates principles of representative design
   a. controls more rigorously for differential selection.
   b. takes more variables into account than a typical experiment.
   c. controls more rigorously for experimenter effects.
   d. sacrifices population validity for increased internal validity.
Answer: b

9. (obj. 4) A useful technique to minimize the effect of experimenter bias on the outcomes of an experiment is for the researcher to
   a. fully inform the experimenters about the study's objectives and hypotheses.
   b. conduct the experiment rather than train experimenters to do so.
   c. train experimenters who are naive about the study to implement the treatments and collect the data.
   d. make the control treatment as desirable as the experimental treatment.
Answer: c

10. (obj. 5) Intact groups often pose a problem when designing experiments because
    a. intact groups cannot be randomly selected from a defined population.
    b. intact groups cannot be assigned to control treatments.
    c. administrators usually are concerned that experiments tend to weaken the cohesiveness of such groups.
    d. individuals within an intact group cannot be randomly assigned to the experimental and control groups.

Answer: d

11. (obj. 6) The one-group pretest-posttest design is best used when
    a. the characteristic that constitutes the dependent variable is relatively stable.
    b. the experimental treatment extends over a relatively long period.
    c. history may function as an extraneous variable.
    d. the control group has not been randomly selected.

Answer: a

12. (obj. 6) Which of the following experimental designs has the best internal validity?
    a. the one-group pretest-posttest design.
    b. the pretest-posttest control-group design.
    c. the time series design.
    d. the one-shot case study.

Answer: b

13. (obj. 6) A researcher designs an experiment in which student teachers are randomly assigned to three treatment groups: twice-weekly supervisory visits, weekly supervisory visits, and supervisory visits every two weeks. This is an example of a
    a. pretest-posttest control-group design.
    b. one-shot case study.
    c. one-group pretest-posttest design.
    d. one-variable multiple-condition design.

Answer: d

14. (obj. 7) Of the following experimental designs, the strongest in external validity is the
    a. one-shot case study.
    b. one-group pretest-posttest design.
    c. posttest-only control-group design.
    d. pretest-posttest control-group design.

Answer: c

15. (obj. 7) The main threat to the external validity of the pretest-posttest control-group design is the
   a. Hawthorne effect.
   b. interaction between history and the experimental treatment.
   c. interaction between time of measurement and the experimental treatment.
   d. interaction between the pretest and the experimental treatment.
Answer: d

16. (obj. 8) What is the preferred statistical technique for analyzing the data from an experiment that employs a pretest-posttest control-group design?
   a. analysis of variance.
   b. analysis of covariance.
   c. two t tests, one comparing the pretest and posttest means of the experimental group and the other comparing the pretest and posttest means of the control group.
   d. a t test comparing the posttest means of the experimental and control groups.
Answer: b

17. (obj. 8) What is the preferred statistical technique for analyzing the data from an experiment that employs a posttest-only control-group design?
   a. a t test comparing the posttest means of the experimental and control groups.
   b. multiple regression.
   c. analysis of covariance.
   d. the correlation ratio.
Answer: a

OPEN-FORM ITEMS

1. (obj. 1) What does it mean to say that an experiment has good internal validity?
Answer:
It means that extraneous variables have been well controlled by the researcher, so that any observed effect on the dependent variable can be attributed solely to the treatment variable.

2. (obj. 1) List and describe five types of extraneous variables that are threats to the internal validity of an experiment.

Answer (any 5 OK):

a. *History*. Treatments extending over a period of time allow variables other than the experimental treatment that happen to be occurring during that time to affect the results.

b. *Maturation*. During the experimental treatment, changes occur that are due to natural developmental changes in the subjects rather than to the treatment.

c. *Testing*. Experience with a pretest can lead to better performance on the posttest.

d. *Instrumentation*. Faulty instruments can lead to apparent changes when no real change has occurred (such as using a posttest that is easier than the pretest).

e. *Differential selection*. The basis for selection of the treatment and control groups is different.

f. *Experimental mortality*. Differential loss of research subjects occurs for reasons that have nothing to do with the remaining sample. For example, students who are doing well may continue with a program while those who are doing poorly drop out, or control group subjects may drop out at a different rate from experimental group subjects.

g. *Statistical regression*. In any test-retest design regression toward the mean can occur for subjects whose scores are at the tails of the score distribution. This phenomenon suggests an apparent change when no real change has occurred. It is a serious problem in studies dealing with extreme groups, such as children with severe learning disabilities.

h. *Selection-maturation interaction*. Groups are selected (i.e., treatment vs. control) that differ in maturation level.

i. *Experimental treatment diffusion*. Members of the control group obtain access to the experimental treatment.

j. *Compensatory rivalry by the control group*. Control group subjects perform beyond their usual level because they perceive that they are in competition with the experimental group.

k. *Compensatory equalization of treatments*. The control group receives goods and services similar to those that are part of the treatment received by the experimental group.

l. *Resentful demoralization of the control group*. Control group subjects become discouraged because they perceive that the experimental group is receiving a desirable treatment that is being withheld from them.

173

3. (obj. 2)
    a.   Describe *pretest sensitization.*
    b.   Is it a threat to the internal or external validity of an experiment?
Answer:
    a.   The pretest can sensitize subjects to the experimental treatment and bring about different results from what would have been obtained if no pretest had been given.
    b.   This is a threat to ecological validity, which is a form of external validity.

4. (obj. 3) Representative design is an attempt to make experiments more representative of the natural environment. What are two recommended approaches for making educational research more representative?
Answer (any 2 OK):
    a.   When appropriate, conduct the research in the actual field setting to which you wish to generalize your findings.
    b.   Incorporate several environmental variations into the design of the experiment. For example, if the purpose is to evaluate a new instructional method, it is advisable to have not one teacher but rather a sample of teachers using it.
    c.   Observe what subjects actually are doing during the experiment. These observations may prove helpful to the researcher in interpreting the experimental results.
    d.   A related technique to *c* above is to observe the social context in which the experiment is being conducted. Certain events that occur in schools or in other educational settings may affect the experimental treatment. If these events are observed and recorded, the research findings should be more interpretable.
    e.   Prepare subjects for the experiment. The typical practice is for researchers to give simple instructions to the subjects and perhaps a few minutes of training prior to the start of an experiment. However, more extensive preparation may be necessary to ensure a smooth transition from subjects' current mental set to the one required by the experimental task.
    f.   Incorporate a control treatment that allows subjects to use their customary approaches to learning.

5. (obj. 4) What are two techniques that a researcher can use to avoid experimenter bias?
Answer:
    a.   Train naive experimenters to work with the research participants.
    b.   Avoid suggesting to the experimenters that one experimental treatment is better than another.

6. (obj. 5) How can randomization be achieved if individuals within intact groups cannot be randomly assigned to the experimental and control groups?
Answer:
Select a sample of intact groups and randomly assign these groups to the experimental and control conditions.

7. (obj. 6)
    a.   What is one advantage of the pretest-posttest control-group design over the posttest-only control-group design?
    b.   What threat to external validity is present in the pretest-posttest control-group design?
Answer:
    a.   (any 1 OK):
        (1) The former design gives the investigator assurance that the treatment groups are initially comparable.
        (2) The former design permits adjusting for initial group differences.
    b.   Pretest sensitization is a threat to the external validity of this design.

8. (obj. 7)
    a.   What is the most important limitation of the one-group pretest-posttest design?
    b.   What kinds of variables can be studied by using this design?
Answer:
    a.   Because there is no control group, the investigator cannot estimate the proportion of the pretest-posttest change that is due to extraneous variables such as history or maturation as compared with the proportion of change due to treatment.
    b.   This design is useful in studying changes in very stable variables, e.g., those for which change is very unlikely in the absence of a specific treatment. Attitudes of adults, for example, have been found to be stable. This design also is appropriate in training studies in which there is almost no chance for subjects to learn the content unless they are trained.

9. (obj. 8) A researcher conducts an experiment that employs a pretest-posttest control-group design. The pretest and the posttest are similar tests of American history. Describe the statistical technique that should be used to analyze the pretest and posttest scores.
Answer:
Use analysis of covariance, assuming its assumptions are satisfied. The posttest mean of the experimental group is compared with the posttest mean of the control group, with the pretest scores as the covariate.

APPLICATION PROBLEMS

Problem 1

Study the following research plan and identify any variables and/or conditions that may pose a threat to the internal validity of the research. Name the most likely threats to internal validity, and explain each briefly in terms of the research plan.

Research plan: The researcher wants to determine the effect of a special reading program on the reading achievement of inner-city children. The study will be longitudinal, extending from the beginning of grade 2 to the end of grade 3. He identifies 50 children who are nonreaders at the end of grade 1; these children will receive the special program. He randomly selects 50 other children in the same school and grade level to serve as a control group. The researcher administers a reading test to both groups at the start of grade 2 and at the end of grade 3. By the end of grade 3, there are 27 children who have remained in the special program and 36 children in the control group. The researcher compares the reading gains of the two groups and finds that each group has gained an average of 1.6 years in reading grade placement.

Sample Answer:

    a. *History.* Over a two-year period, other events could have influenced the reading performance of the subjects. These events may not have been the same, because the treatment cases were nonreaders while the controls were randomly selected.

    b. *Statistical regression.* Because the treatment group was below average at the start of the experiment while the controls were randomly selected, the posttest scores of the treatment group probably would regress upward, while no regression would occur for the controls as a group.

    c. *Differential selection.* The basis for selecting the treatment and the control groups was different.

    d. *Experimental mortality.* The greater loss of subjects from the treatment group could have biased the sample.

    e. *Selection-maturation interaction.* The treatment subjects could have been less mature when selected, because selection was on a different basis for the two groups.

    f. *Maturation.* Poorer first-grade performance could have indicated lower maturation for the treatment group.

    g. *Pretest effect.* This is not very likely to have occurred.

Problem 2

A researcher is planning an experiment to test the effectiveness of the discussion method at the high school level. One teacher has agreed to use the discussion method in her class several times a week for a semester. Another teacher has agreed to teach the same content but without using the discussion method. The researcher will collect the following data: student scores on an achievement test and on a scale measuring attitudes toward the instruction. What recommendations can you offer to improve the representativeness of this experimental design?

Sample Answer:

    a.   Instead of one teacher each in the experimental and control treatments, recruit a sample of teachers to be in each treatment. The courses represented in each treatment (e.g., English or history) also might be varied.

    b.   Plan for observation of in-class activities during the experimental period. The observational data may help in the interpretation of the results.

    c.   Provide a reasonable amount of preparation for students who are to be in the treatment involving discussion. They may be unfamiliar with the discussion method and thus they may react negatively to its introduction into the curriculum unless they are adequately prepared beforehand.

Problem 3

A researcher wants to test the effectiveness of providing high school students with a note-taking outline of each chapter that they are assigned to read in a history class. She has permission to conduct the experiment with two history classes, each containing 30 students. She randomly forms two groups within each class: The experimental group receives a note-taking outline each time it is assigned a chapter, while the control group receives the same assignment but not a note-taking outline. On the basis of this information, what flaw has the researcher introduced into the experimental design?

Sample Answer:

This experimental design creates the threat of experimental treatment diffusion. It will be difficult to ensure that none of the students in the control group will try to obtain the note-taking outline (which is the experimental treatment) from a classmate who is in the experimental group. If some of the control-group students obtain the outline, the experiment is no longer a pure comparison between two types of experimental treatment.

Problem 4

A researcher is planning to test the effectiveness of a new reading program. A sample of 40 teachers distributed evenly among five schools in one school district has volunteered to use the program for a semester. Using only this sample, the researcher wishes to form two equivalent groups, one of which will participate in the special program while the other receives the regular program. State methods for achieving equivalence between the groups through random assignment.

Sample Answer:

    a.   One method is to assign teachers randomly to the experimental and control treatments.

    b.   Another method is to assign students randomly in each classroom to the experimental and control groups.

Problem 5

A researcher wants to determine whether students learn more when they take unannounced, pop quizzes or regularly scheduled, announced quizzes. The measure of learning will be a 50-item achievement test on the content covered in a semester-long course. Describe the steps involved in designing and conducting an experiment based on this information.

Sample Answer:

    a.   Randomly assign some classes to the experimental treatment group (pop quizzes) and other classes to the alternate treatment group (announced quizzes).

    b.   Administer the achievement test as a pretest to both groups at the beginning of the semester.

    c.   Implement the two treatments: pop quizzes and announced quizzes. Check for treatment fidelity.

    d.   Administer the achievement test as a posttest to both groups at the end of the semester.

    e.   Use analysis of covariance to analyze the data. The posttest scores are the dependent variable and the pretest scores are the covariate.

TEACHING ACTIVITIES

Activity 1

Identify a research article that describes an experimental study that employed one of the designs covered in chapter 12 of the textbook. Have all students read the study as a homework assignment and then discuss in class the technical aspects of the study's research methodology and the study's strengths and weaknesses.

Activity 2

Have students design an experiment using one of the more powerful designs covered in the chapter, namely, the pretest-posttest control-group design or the one-variable multiple-condition design. In class, take students through the following steps in creating the design:

a.   Have the class reach consensus on an experimental treatment to be investigated.

b.   Create an appropriate control-group condition.

c.   Consider possible threats to the internal validity of the experiment and steps that can be taken to minimize or avoid the threats.

d.   Consider how the experiment can be designed to enhance its external validity.

e.   Consider features of representative design that can be incorporated into the experiment.

f.   Specify one or more tests that can be administered to measure the dependent variable(s)

g.   Design a technique for checking treatment fidelity.

h.   Create hypothetical pretest and posttest means for the experimental and control groups, and select the most appropriate statistical technique(s) for analyzing the data.

i.   If students have read about research designs in other chapters of the textbook, ask them whether it would be possible to investigate the effects of the experimental treatment using one of these other designs. If the answer is yes, ask students to compare the advantages and disadvantages of their experimental design with those of the other type of research design.

Activity 3

If you know a researcher who is doing or has done an experiment involving one of the designs covered in this chapter, invite this person to be a guest presenter. Ask the researcher to discuss why she chose to do an experiment, problems that arose in conducting it, how she handled these problems, what she learned by doing the experiment, and what direction future research on the phenomenon might take.

Note: The phrase in parentheses following the item number for both closed-form and open-form items, for example, 1. (obj. 3), refers to the textbook chapter objective to which the item is keyed.

CLOSED-FORM ITEMS

1. (obj. 1) The statistical procedure that typically is used to analyze data from an experiment that employs a nonequivalent control-group design is
   a. analysis of variance.
   b. analysis of covariance.
   c. a *t* test for independent means.
   d. a *t* test for correlated means.
Answer: b

2. (obj. 2)   0   X   0

$$\overline{0} \; \overline{-} \; \overline{0}$$

The graph above describes the
   a. nonequivalent control-group design.
   b. time series design.
   c. counterbalanced design.
   d. static-group comparison design.
Answer: a

3. (obj. 3) The main threat to the internal validity of the static-group comparison design is that
   a. the pretest may sensitize subjects to the experimental treatment.
   b. this design does not include a control group.
   c. posttest differences between groups may be due to preexisting group differences rather than to the experimental treatment.
   d. the experimental treatment may diffuse to the control group.
Answer: c

4. (obj. 4) Match each example with the type of treatment variable it represents.
   __ 1. Traditional vs. innovative method of teaching reading.
   __ 2. Male vs. female students.
   __ 3. High vs. low scorers on an achievement test.
   __ 4. High vs. low socioeconomic level of a school's student population.
   __ 5. Vocational vs. academic curriculum.
       a. Potentially manipulable aspects of the environment.
       b. Relatively fixed aspects of the environment.
       c. Manipulated variables.
       d. Response characteristics of research participants.
       e. Organismic characteristics of research participants.
Answer: 1=c, 2=e, 3=d, 4=b, 5=a

5. (obj. 4) Students' scores on a test are an example of
   a. a manipulated variable.
   b. an organismic characteristic of subjects.
   c. a response characteristic of subjects.
   d. a relatively fixed aspect of the environment.
Answer: c

6. (obj. 5) In a factorial experiment, the researcher
   a. analyzes the treatment variable into two or more factors.
   b. analyzes the dependent variable into two or more factors.
   c. determines the effect of one treatment variable on a dependent variable.
   d. determines the effect of two or more treatment variables on a dependent variable.
Answer: d

7. (obj. 5) Aptitude-treatment-interaction research is concerned with
   a. the exploration of matches between learner characteristics and different
       instructional methods.
   b. the use of the experimental method to develop aptitude tests.
   c. the combined effects of response and organismic characteristics on research
       participants' performance.
   d. whether a combination of treatments can affect research participants' aptitude.
Answer: a

8. (obj. 5) A 3 X 2 factorial design means that there are
    a.   six interaction effects.
    b.   three levels of one factor and two levels of another factor.
    c.   six factors.
    d.   three factors, two of which are manipulated.
Answer: b

9. The main purpose of the Solomon four-group design is to determine the presence of
    a.   experimenter bias.
    b.   an aptitude-treatment interaction.
    c.   an attribute-treatment interaction.
    d.   pretest sensitization.
Answer: d

10. (obj. 6) The single-subject experiment is particularly well suited to
    a.   survey research methodology.
    b.   research on behavior modification.
    c.   use in cross-cultural studies.
    d.   sociological research.
Answer: b

11. (obj. 6) Careful training of observers, operational definition of behaviors, and control of observer bias are all used to ensure ___ in single-subject experiments.
    a.   precise description of the experimental conditions
    b.   baseline and treatment stability
    c.   reliable observation
    d.   all of the above
Answer: c

12. (obj. 6) Because of the need for repeated measurements in single-subject designs, it is important to
    a.   obtain measurements of behavioral products rather than behavior.
    b.   standardize the measurement procedure.
    c.   discontinue treatment as soon as improvement occurs.
    d.   use participant observation whenever possible.
Answer: b

13. (obj. 7) The A-B-A-B design
    a. avoids the problem of ending an experiment with withdrawal or reversal of the treatment.
    b. avoids the possibility that an observed treatment effect will be dependent on the particular baseline conditions included in the experiment.
    c. has lower internal validity than an A-B-A design.
    d. all of the above.
Answer: a

14. (obj. 7) Conditions other than the naturally occurring target behavior are used as controls in
    a. an A-B design.
    b. an A-B-A design.
    c. an A-B-A-B design.
    d. a multiple-baseline design.
Answer: d

15. (obj. 7) An appropriate method for analyzing single-case data is
    a. inspection of the graphed data.
    b. descriptive statistics.
    c. inferential statistics.
    d. all of the above.
Answer: d

16. (obj. 8) The A-B-A-B design
    a. is the best single-case design for studying multiple treatments.
    b. ends with treatment reversal.
    c. yields findings about treatment effects that are dependent on the particular baseline conditions included in the experiment.
    d. is low in internal validity.
Answer: c

17. (obj. 9) If the range of difficulty of test items is limited, the test may be subject to
    a. statistical regression.
    b. instrumentation effects.
    c. a lack of replicability.
    d. a ceiling effect.
Answer: d

18. (obj. 9) An appropriate technique for determining the statistical significance of pretest-posttest change in experiments is
    a. an analysis of variance for repeated measures.
    b. the *t* test for independent means.
    c. the *t* test for correlated means.
    d. a Mann-Whitney *U* test.
Answer: a

OPEN-FORM ITEMS

1. (obj. 1) Describe a statistical technique that can be used to reduce initial group differences resulting from nonrandom assignment of subjects to the experimental and control treatments.
Answer:
Analysis of covariance can be used. The posttest scores are the dependent variable and the pretest scores are the covariate.

2. (obj. 2)
    a. What is the main difference between a static-group comparison design and a nonequivalent control-group design?
    b. Which design is stronger in internal validity, and why?
Answer:
    a. The nonequivalent control-group design includes both a pretest and a posttest for the experimental and control groups, but the static-group comparison design includes only a posttest.
    b. The nonequivalent control-group design is stronger in internal validity, because the availability of pretest scores makes it possible to assess whether pre-existing group differences can be ruled out as a cause of observed effects on the dependent variable.

3. (obj. 3)
    a. What threat to external validity is controlled by the Solomon four-group design?
    b. How is the threat to external validity controlled by this design?
Answer:
    a. Pretest sensitization.
    b. This external validity threat is controlled by including one treatment group that is given a pretest and another treatment group that is not given a pretest. A comparison of these groups indicates whether the pretest had an effect on the dependent variable.

4. (obj. 4) In experiments involving a factorial design, five types of independent variables may be employed. Name and describe three of these types of independent variables.

Answer (any 3 OK):

  a. Manipulated variables, such as teaching method, assignable at will by the experimenter.

  b. Potentially manipulable aspects, such as school subject studied, that the experimenter might assign in some varied way to the research participants but rarely does.

  c. Relatively fixed aspects of the environment, such as community or school or socioeconomic level, not under the direct control of the experimenter but serving as explicit bases for stratification in the experiment.

  d. Organismic characteristics of the research participants, such as age, height, weight, and gender.

  e. Response characteristics of the research participants, such as scores on various tests.

5. (obj. 5) Using a factorial design, a researcher conducted an experiment to determine how prior vocabulary knowledge and a new reading program influence students' reading comprehension. The new reading program is the experimental treatment, and the existing reading program is the control treatment.

  a. Identify what would be a main effect in this experiment, and define what is meant by a main effect.

  b. Identify what would be an interaction effect in this experiment, and define what is meant by an interaction effect.

Answer:

  a. The type of reading program is a main effect, and vocabulary knowledge also is a main effect. A main effect is an observed effect of an independent variable on the dependent variable.

  b. An interaction effect would be the finding that the effect of the type of reading program on reading comprehension is influenced by students' prior vocabulary knowledge. An interaction effect occurs when the effect of one independent variable on the dependent variable is influenced by another independent variable.

6. (obj. 5)

  a. What is the purpose of attribute-treatment interaction (ATI) research?

  b. What type of experimental design is employed in ATI research?

Answer:

  a. The purpose of ATI research is to determine whether the effects of different instructional methods are influenced by the cognitive or personality characteristics of the learners.

  b. ATI studies employ a factorial design because there are at least two independent variables, such as instructional method and learner characteristics.

7. (obj. 6) Why is the A-B-A-B design considered more acceptable from an ethical standpoint than the A-B-A design?
Answer:
These designs are used for the most part to reduce an undesirable behavior or increase a desirable behavior. In the A-B-A design the treatment that brings about favorable change is withdrawn, returning the research participant to the original condition. In the A-B-A-B design the treatment (B) is reintroduced, which leaves the research participant in the improved condition.

8. (obj. 7) What is the main difference between an A-B-A design and a multiple-baseline design in a single-case experiment?
Answer:
An A-B-A experiment uses the natural occurrence of the target behavior as a control condition for assessing treatment effects, whereas a multiple-baseline experiment uses other conditions (e.g., different cases or multiple target behaviors) as a control condition.

9. (obj. 8) Which of the two single-subject designs, A-B or A-B-A, has superior internal validity? Why?
Answer:
The A-B-A design has superior internal validity, because if withdrawal of the treatment (i.e., the second A) results in return of the research participant's behavior to the original baseline (i.e., the first A) it provides strong evidence that the treatment actually caused the change in the dependent variable brought about in condition B. In the A-B design, the change in the dependent variable could have been brought about by extraneous variables such as history or maturation, and the effect of extraneous variables cannot be separated from treatment effects.

10. (obj. 9) Suppose an achievement test measures various calculus skills. If this test is administered to the research participants before and after an experiment, what problem is created by computing a gain score (i.e., posttest score minus pretest score) for each participant?
Answer:
A particular gain score may have different meanings for different participants in the experiment. For example, one participant may have made a gain of five points because of a large improvement in one calculus skill, whereas another participant may have made a gain of five points because of small improvements in several other calculus skills.

11. (obj. 9) Describe two alternatives to a a gain score in analyzing research data from a correlational or experimental study that included administration of a pretest and a posttest.
Answer (any 2 OK):

a. Part correlation, in which the gain scores are correlated with another variable after adjusting the gain scores so that the research participants' pretest scores are partialled out (i.e., held constant).

b. Multiple regression, in which the pretest scores are entered into the multiple regression equation first so that their effect on the posttest scores is partialled out.

c. Analysis of covariance, in which the posttest means of an experimental group and a control group are compared, with the pretest scores serving as a covariate.

d. Analysis of variance for repeated measures, in which a determination is made as to whether the pretest-posttest difference for the experimental group is reliably different from the pretest-posttest difference for the control group.

APPLICATION PROBLEMS

Problem 1

A researcher wishes to determine which of two types of staff development is more effective. The administrators of a school district agree to the experiment, and all the teachers in two high schools agree to participate and to take the pretest and posttest. However, the administrators insist that the teachers cannot be randomly assigned to the staff development programs. All teachers in one high school must participate in program A, and all teachers in the other high school must participate in program B.

a. If the researcher agrees to this condition, what type of experimental design must she use and why?

b. What is the main threat to internal validity in this type of experimental design, and how can it be handled?

Sample Answer:

a. The researcher will need to conduct a quasi-experiment that employs a nonequivalent control-group design, because the assignment of teachers to the two treatments is nonrandom.

b. The main threat to the internal validity of this type of experiment is that the two groups of teachers may differ on one or more characteristics prior to the experiment. These characteristics rather than the treatment variable (i.e., type of staff development) may be responsible for any observed effect on the dependent variable. To control for initial group differences the researcher can use analysis of covariance, which will statistically equate the two groups on the pretest administration of the dependent variable.

Problem 2

A researcher plans to test the effectiveness of self-paced instruction vs. conventional instruction for male and female students of varying levels of ability. There are a total of 150 students: 60 boys and 90 girls. Within each of these groups (boys and girls), there are an equal number of high-, middle-, and low-ability students. Make a chart that illustrates the experimental design for this research project, and show the number of students in each experimental group. Also, list each interaction effect that can be analyzed.

Sample Answer:

Ability	Conventional Instruction		Traditional Instruction	
	Boys	Girls	Boys	Girls
High	10	15	10	15
Middle	10	15	10	15
Low	10	15	10	15

Interaction effects:

A X B
A X C
B X C
A X B X C

Where:

A = treatment.
B = gender of student.
C = ability level of student.

Problem 3

A new program has been developed to increase students' speed and accuracy in simple arithmetic computations. You have been asked by the school district's curriculum specialist to evaluate its effectiveness. One of the first decisions you must make is whether to use a group or a single-subject experimental design. What questions could you ask the curriculum specialist about the program and the purpose of the experiment to determine whether a group or single-subject design is more appropriate, and what is the purpose of each question?

Sample Answer:

    a.   Is the curriculum specialist more interested in the learning of individual students or in the learning of students as a group? Single-subject designs focus on the individual learner, whereas group designs focus on group trends.

    b.   Is it possible to give students many tests of the computational skills? Single-subject designs require frequent measurement of the same variable.

    c.   Is it possible to meet the requirements of an A-B-A design or of a multiple-baseline design in the classes that will participate in the experiment? An A-B-A design (e.g., reinstating baseline conditions after withdrawal of treatment) or a multiple-baseline design (e.g., changing one computational skill at a time) each impose unique requirements on the participants in an experiment. The researcher needs to determine which research design is more acceptable to them.

Problem 4

A researcher conducted an experiment in which he administered an arithmetic test before and after students had participated in a new individualized curriculum. Parallel forms of the test were used as the pretest and posttest, and the range of possible scores was 0-100 on each. In analyzing data from the experiment, the researcher found that students in the lowest quartile on the pretest ($M = 15.5$) made a good gain (posttest $M = 37.6$), whereas students in the highest quartile on the pretest ($M = 83.7$) declined slightly (posttest $M = 80.1$). From these differences in gain scores, he concluded that the new curriculum is more effective for students of low ability than for students of high ability. What are two other interpretations that could be made of the differences in gain scores?

Sample Answer:

    a.   Regression toward the mean could have occurred.

    b.   Students in the highest quartile may have made a substantial gain but it was not reflected in the posttest due to a ceiling effect; that is, the posttest may not have measured the entire range of possible achievement for the particular variables of concern.

TEACHING ACTIVITIES

Activity 1
Identify a research article that describes an experimental study that employed one of the designs covered in chapter 13 of the textbook. Have all students read the study as a homework assignment and then discuss in class the technical aspects of the study's research methodology and the study's strengths and weaknesses.

Activity 2
You can have students practice designing an experiment using one of the more powerful designs covered in the chapter, such as a nonequivalent control-group design, a factorial design, or an A-B-A design. You can give students a research problem for which one of these designs is appropriate, or you can have them generate both the problem and the design. You can have students follow each step for the design as specified in the textbook. Because there is no single correct procedure for each step, students can generate alternate procedures for each step and consider their strengths and weaknesses.

Activity 3
If you know a researcher who is doing or has done an experiment involving one of the designs covered in this chapter, invite this person to be a guest presenter. Ask the researcher to discuss why she chose to do an experiment, any problems that arose in conducting it, how she handled these problems, what she learned by doing the experiment, and what direction future research on the phenomenon might take.

CHAPTER 14
CASE STUDY RESEARCH

Note: The phrase in parentheses following the item number for both closed-form and open-form items, for example, 1. (obj. 3), refers to the textbook chapter objective to which the item is keyed.

CLOSED-FORM ITEMS

1. (obj. 1) Which of the following is characteristic of qualitative case study research?
    a. the study of particular instances of a phenomenon
    b. the in-depth study of a phenomenon.
    c. the study of a phenomenon in its natural context.
    d. all of the above.
Answer: d

2. (obj. 2) A case study in which the researcher relates differences in how adults cope with reading comprehension problems to a theory of intellectual development most clearly illustrates the purpose of ___ in case study research.
    a. description
    b. explanation
    c. confirmation
    d. evaluation
Answer: b

3. (obj. 3) The primary aim of thick description is to
    a. compile as many objective facts about a phenomenon as possible.
    b. illustrate communalities among a wide variety of phenomena.
    c. provide information to assess the worth of a phenomenon.
    d. re-create the context within which a particular phenomenon is situated.
Answer: d

4. (obj. 3) Rayna was late for school eight times in October, and gave the teacher varying explanations for the cause of her tardiness. A case study researcher is likely to describe this aspect of the case as a
    a. theme.
    b. construct.
    c. pattern.
    d. phenomenon.
Answer: a

5. (obj. 4) The key issue in selecting the case for a case study is to
   a. decide what phenomenon you want to be able to say something about at the end of the study.
   b. construct specifications for a case that would reflect the phenomenon to an extreme extent.
   c. find gatekeepers who have access to a range of possible candidates for cases.
   d. identify a field setting in which the researcher already is a participant.

Answer: a

6. (obj. 4) Case selection typically involves all but which of the following?
   a. Specifying the phenomenon of interest.
   b. Defining a unit of analysis.
   c. Deciding the focus on which data collection will concentrate.
   d. Determining the population to which the results can be generalized.

Answer: d

7. (obj. 5) The study of multiple cases rather than a single case
   a. requires the identification of more than one focus of investigation.
   b. provides a better learning opportunity for the beginning researcher.
   c. permits exploration of systematic relationships among aspects of the phenomenon.
   d. requires the use of theoretical or literal replication.

Answer: c

8. (obj. 6) Case study researchers are more likely than traditional quantitative researchers to
   a. play a major role in the collection of research data.
   b. formulate their research problems in relation to prior theory.
   c. pay considerable attention to obtaining permissions from the research site.
   d. select a research problem of personal interest to them.

Answer: a

9. (obj. 7) Case study researchers who base their research on ecological ethics
   a. aim to produce the greatest good for the greatest number of people.
   b. judge the morality of their decisions by whether they reflect a caring attitude toward others.
   c. refer to absolute values in assessing whether they are behaving ethically.
   d. consider the participants' culture as the major determinant of the morality of the researchers' actions.

Answer: d

10. (obj. 7) In securing permission to collect data in a research site, the case study researcher should
    a. dress and speak more formally than usual.
    b. describe the code of ethics that the researcher espouses.
    c. contact people within the site whom the researcher knows personally.
    d. work with gatekeepers at the site.
Answer: d

11. (obj. 8) Most experts believe that a researcher's disclosure of personal information about himself to case study participants
    a. is necessary for obtaining their cooperation.
    b. has minimal effect on the research findings.
    c. tends to inhibit the research participants' expression of their own feelings and experiences.
    d. is a violation of research ethics.
Answer: b

12. (obj. 8) In most case studies, researchers
    a. use one method of data collection.
    b. begin data analysis before ending data collection.
    c. use contact summary sheets instead of taking field notes.
    d. do not decide the form for presenting the case study until all the data are analyzed.
Answer: b

13. (obj. 8) Thinking "finish-to-start" in doing a case study involves
    a. analyzing the data before ending data collection.
    b. predetermining the information to be sought from each contact or document.
    c. predetermining the relative emphasis to be given to description, analysis, and interpretation in the case study report.
    d. developing a timeline that is anchored by the date when data collection must end.
Answer: c

14. (obj. 9) Exhaustion of sources, saturation of categories, emergence of regularities, and overextension all are
    a. criteria for deciding when to end the data-collection stage of a case study.
    b. topics that should be explored in a subjectivity audit.
    c. examples of the types of themes that might characterize a case.
    d. criteria for judging the interpretive validity of a case study.
Answer: a

15. (obj. 9) A case study researcher probably should collect additional data rather than end data collection when
   a. new information far from the central core of viable coding categories is received.
   b. the data being collected reflect the emergence of regularities.
   c. key informants have provided minimal information.
   d. all of the above.

Answer: c

16. (obj. 10) Structural analysis of qualitative data involves the researcher's
   a. inferences about the meaning of data segments.
   b. identification of patterns inherent in textual elements.
   c. use of intuition to portray the phenomena being studied.
   d. coding of the degree of occurrence of particular variables in each case.

Answer: b

17. (obj. 10) Text retrievers are used in case study research to
   a. identify all data fields that have been assigned to a given code.
   b. list the location and frequency of all the words in a document.
   c. determine whether specific coding categories overlap.
   d. segment the database prior to analysis.

Answer: b

18. (obj. 10) The qualitative research tradition of educational connoisseurship and criticism best illustrates the method of
   a. structural analysis.
   b. constant comparison.
   c. reflective analysis.
   d. interpretational analysis.

Answer: c

19. (obj. 11) The main difference between a positivist and an interpretive researcher's orientation to determining the validity of case study findings is whether the researcher
   a. seeks to demonstrate a causal relationship between the variables being investigated.
   b. believes there is an objective reality to be discovered.
   c. triangulates data-collection methods, data sources, analysts, or theories.
   d. asks members of the sample who were studied to check the accuracy of the report.

Answer: b

20. (obj. 11) The extent to which a measure in a case study correctly operationalizes the concepts being studied is an indicator of the extent to which the study's design reflects
   a. construct validity.
   b. internal validity.
   c. external validity.
   d. reliability.

Answer: a

21. (obj. 12) Outlier analysis is used in case study research to determine
   a. the extent to which the emic and etic perspectives of the phenomenon being studied are congruent.
   b. why particular members of the sample disagree with the case study's conclusions.
   c. whether the findings for extreme cases are consistent with those for other cases.
   d. why some data for a case diverge from other data for the same case.

Answer: c

22. (obj. 12) Asking the individuals studied for more information to reconcile discrepancies in the case study report is an example of
   a. member checking.
   b. triangulation.
   c. pattern matching.
   d. representativeness checking.

Answer: a

23. (obj. 13) Case study findings are likely to be generalizable in all but which of the following situations?
   a. The researcher studied a typical case.
   b. The research was based on grounded theory.
   c. A random sample from the unit of analysis was studied.
   d. The report readers' field setting is similar to that described in the case study.

Answer: b

24. (obj. 14) Reflective reporting of a case study is most appropriate when the researcher
   a. made an interpretational analysis of the case study data.
   b. wants to maintain an objective stance.
   c. wants to have her voice strongly present in the report.
   d. wants to display how bits of information relate to each other.

Answer: c

25. (obj. 14) Researchers who report their case studies in the form of fiction, poetry, drama, satire, or other literary genres usually
   a. have a postmodern sensibility.
   b. are using an interpretational reporting style.
   c. have minimal concern for demonstrating the validity of their findings.
   d. have studied a single case.
Answer: a

26. (obj. 15) A disadvantage of the case study method compared to traditional quantitative research designs is that
   a. it requires the use of a computer for coding the data.
   b. the case on which the study will focus can change late in the research process.
   c. it provides a less adequate basis for action than a quantitative research report.
   d. it is difficult to generalize the findings to other situations.
Answer: d

OPEN-FORM ITEMS

1. (obj. 1) Describe the four defining characteristics of a case study.
Answer:
   a. It involves the study of phenomena by focusing on specific instances of the phenomenon, that is, cases.
   b. An in-depth study is made of each case.
   c. The phenomenon is studied as it occurs in its natural context.
   d. The participants' perspective (that is, the emic perspective) of the phenomenon is sought.

2. (obj. 2) Describe the three purposes for which case studies typically are carried out.
Answer:
   a. Description of the phenomena in sufficient detail to re-create them and their context, along with the meanings and intentions inherent in the situation.
   b. Explanation of the phenomena, with a focus on the relationships observed among them and the causal patterns within those relationships.
   c. Evaluation of specific instances of a phenomenon, in which the researcher uses case study findings to make judgments about their worth or value.

3. (obj. 3) Explain what is meant by thick description in case study research.
Answer:
Thick description involves the researcher's depiction and conceptualization of a phenomenon in sufficient detail to re-create it in its natural context and to convey the meanings and intentions inherent in that context.

4. (obj. 3) Explain (a) the meaning of a pattern in case study research and (b) the difference between a relational pattern and a causal pattern.
Answer:
    a.   A pattern refers to the observation of a systematic relationship between one type of variation and another type of variation in a case study.
    b.   A relational pattern involves a relationship in which no claim is made that one variation caused the other, while a causal pattern involves a relationship in which the researcher claims that one variation did cause the other.

5. (obj. 4) A researcher decides to study the educational philosophies of three teachers out of ten teachers in one school district whom a key informant identified as outstanding instructional leaders. What are (a) the phenomenon, (b) the focus, (c) the unit of analysis, and (d) the case or cases in this case study?
Answer:
    a.   The phenomenon of interest is instructional leadership.
    b.   The focus is the educational philosophy of outstanding instructional leaders.
    c.   The unit of analysis is the ten teachers identified as outstanding instructional leaders within the selected field setting.
    d.   The case is the three teachers whom the researcher selects as his sample for the case study, and each of these three teachers also can be described as a separate case.

6. (obj. 5) State one advantage and one disadvantage of studying multiple cases rather than a single case in a case study.
Answer:
An advantage of studying multiple cases is that the researcher can compare cases and discover systematic relationships among the phenomena that they involve. A disadvantage is that the study of multiple cases reduces the total attention that the researcher has available to give to a single case.

7. (obj. 6) Describe the role of the qualitative case study researcher in data collection, and typical activities that this role involves.
Answer:
As the primary "measuring instrument," the researcher carries out data collection and becomes personally involved in the phenomenon being studied. Typical activities in this role are interacting closely with research participants, attending social events in the field setting, and using empathy and intuition to grasp the meaning of the phenomenon as experienced by those in the setting.

8. (obj. 6) Name and explain two of the ethical stances from which researchers can judge the morality of their decisions and actions in a case study.
Answer (any 2 OK):
    a.   Utilitarian ethics considers the consequences of the researcher's decisions and actions on all the people who are affected by them.
    b.   Deontological ethics considers absolute values such as honesty, justice, fairness, or respect for others.
    c.   Relational ethics considers whether the decisions and actions reflect a caring attitude toward others.
    d.   Ecological ethics considers the meaning of these decisions and actions as perceived in the context of the research participants' culture and the larger social systems of which they are a part.

9. (obj. 7) Name two skills a researcher needs in order to gain entry to a field setting and enlist the cooperation of case study participants.
Answer (any 2 OK):
    a.   The ability to identify an appropriate field site.
    b.   The ability to work with gatekeepers at the site to obtain necessary permissions.
    c.   A respectful and cordial manner of relating to prospective research participants.
    d.   A personal appearance with which research participants feel comfortable.

10. (obj. 8) Give one reason why a researcher might collect both qualitative and quantitative data in a case study.
Answer (any 1 OK):
    a.   Using more than one method of data collection can enhance the validity of case study findings.
    b.   Quantitative data are particularly helpful for arriving at findings that can be generalized to other individuals or situations.
    c.   The two types of data put the phenomenon being investigated into a more complete context.

11. (obj. 9) Describe two theoretical criteria that a researcher should consider in deciding when it is appropriate to end data collection for a case study.
Answer (any 2 OK):

a. Exhaustion of sources, meaning that the researcher senses that little more relevant information can be gained from further contact with the data sources.

b. Saturation of categories, meaning that the categories used to code the data appear to be definitively established and continuing data collection produces only tiny increments of new information relative to the effort expended.

c. Emergence of regularities, meaning that sufficient consistency has been discovered in the data for the researcher to conclude that the constructs that have been generated to represent the phenomena are sufficient.

d. Overextension, meaning that any new information coming in appears to be far removed from the central core of viable categories that have emerged and does not contribute significantly to the emergence of other viable categories.

12. (obj. 10) Define and describe the steps in the approach to analyzing case study data called interpretational analysis.
Answer:
In interpretational analysis, the researcher infers constructs, themes, and patterns from the case study data to describe and explain the phenomenon being studied. It involves the following steps:

a. Selecting or developing a category system that is appropriate for describing aspects of the phenomenon.

b. Dividing the database into segments and coding each segment for the categories that fit it.

c. Grouping all the segments pertaining to each category by the method of constant comparison and, if desired, determining the inter-rater reliability of the coding system.

d. Drawing conclusions about the constructs, themes, and patterns that are salient, and about their generalizability across cases if a multiple-case design has been used.

13. (obj. 10) Describe one difference between structural analysis and reflective analysis as approaches to analyzing case study data.
Answer (any 1 OK):

a. In structural analysis the researcher looks for patterns (e.g. the occurrence of specific textual elements) that are inherent in the data, while in reflective analysis the researcher uses subjective judgment to characterize the phenomenon.

b. Structural analysis often involves the generation of frequency counts of various data elements (e.g., individual words or phrases), while in reflective analysis it is not possible to specify standard procedures.

14. (obj. 11) What is the main difference between positivist and interpretive approaches to determining the validity of case study findings?
Answer:
Case study researchers who are positivists claim that objective knowledge about the world is possible, and thus express a view about determining the validity and reliability of research findings that is similar to the view of quantitative researchers. Researchers who subscribe to the interpretive approach apply different criteria to determine the value of case study findings, and they tend to use concepts such as plausibility, authenticity, credibility, and relevance instead of validity and reliability.

15. (obj. 11) Describe one of the criteria used by case study researchers who subscribe to a positivist philosophy of scientific inquiry to judge the quality of case study design.
Answer (any 1 OK):
   a. Construct validity is the extent to which a measure used in a case study correctly operationalizes the concepts being studied.
   b. Internal validity is the extent to which the researcher has demonstrated a causal relationship between X and Y by showing that other plausible factors could not have caused Y. (This criterion is not applicable to descriptive case study research, which does not seek to identify causal patterns in phenomena.)
   c. External validity is the extent to which the findings of a case study can be generalized to other similar cases.
   d. Reliability is the extent to which other researchers would arrive at similar results if they studied the same case, using the same procedures, as the first researcher.

16. (obj. 12) Describe one of the criteria used to judge the interpretive validity of case study findings, that is, the credibility of the interpretive researcher's knowledge claims.
Answer (any 1 OK):
   a. Usefulness refers to whether the case study findings enlighten those who read the report, help to liberate those being studied or others, or otherwise serve to benefit some group or individual.
   b. Contextual completeness refers to the comprehensiveness of the researcher's contextualization of the case study phenomena (e.g., their history, the participants' activities and perceptions, and the social rules that guide participants' behavior).
   c. Researcher positioning refers to the researcher's demonstration of sensitivity in how he relates to the situation being studied (e.g., his role relationships to those in the field setting, his beliefs, and his personal characteristics).
   d. Reporting style refers to the style in which the researcher conveys case study findings to readers in order to achieve verisimilitude, that is, a style that leads readers to perceive the reconstruction of participants' phenomenological reality as credible and authentic.
(Note: You may also wish to give credit for any of the remaining eight additional procedures for determining validity and reliability described in chapter 14.)

17. (obj. 12) What is the meaning of *triangulation* in case study research, and what is its relevance to judgments of the validity of research findings?
Answer:
Triangulation is the process of using multiple data-collection methods, data sources, analysts, or theories in collecting, analyzing, and drawing conclusions from case study data. It increases the validity of case study findings by eliminating biases that might result from relying on only one data-collection method, source, analyst, or theory.

18. (obj. 12) Describe two types of documentation that might be included in an audit trail to demonstrate the validity of case study findings.
Answer (any 2 OK):
    a. The source and method of recording the raw data.
    b. The data reduction and analysis products.
    c. The products of the data reconstruction and synthesis.
    d. Process notes.
    e. Materials relating to the researchers' intentions, decisions, and dispositions.
    f. Information about instrument development.

19. (obj. 13) Describe one procedure that a researcher can use to increase the probability that case study findings can be generalized.
Answer (any 1 OK):
    a. Select a case that clearly is typical of the phenomenon in which one is interested.
    b. If a unit of analysis has been defined, select a random sample of individuals within this unit of analysis for intensive data collection and analysis.
    c. Place the responsibility for generalizing case study findings on the readers or users of those findings, and write the report so as to help them determine the generalizability of the findings.

20. (obj. 13) Describe one strategy that a researcher can use to help the readers of a case study report determine the generalizability of the findings to other situations.
Answer (any 1 OK):
    a. Provide a thick description of the participants and contexts that make up the case.
    b. Address the issue of how representative the selected case or cases are of the general phenomenon being investigated.
    c. If a multiple-case design was used, conduct a cross-case analysis to provide information about whether the results for different cases constitute a literal or theoretical replication of the findings.

21. (obj. 14) Name one of the primary characteristics of reflective reporting as an approach to writing reports of case studies.
Answer (any 1 OK):

    a. The author uses literary devices (e.g., direct quotes, story telling, or various literary genres like poetry or drama) to bring the case alive for the reader.

    b. There is a strong presence of the researcher's personal voice in the report.

22. (obj. 14) Name one of the primary characteristics of analytic reporting as an approach to writing reports of case studies.
Answer (any 1 OK):

    a. The author uses an objective writing style, that is, the researcher's voice is silent or subdued.

    b. The report follows a conventional organization of topics to be covered, corresponding to a traditional research report.

23. (Obj. 14) Name one other method for reflective reporting of a case study besides the extensive use of direct quotes.
Answer (any 1 OK):

    a. Fiction.
    b. Poetry.
    c. Drama.
    d. Oral readings.
    e. Comedy.
    f. Satire.
    g. Visual presentations.

24. (obj. 15) Describe one advantage and one disadvantage of case study research as compared to other research methods.

Answer (any 1 from each set OK):

Advantages

a. Its use of thick description brings the case to life in a way that is not possible with the statistical methods of quantitative research.

b. The detail in a case study gives readers a better basis for developing theories, designing educational interventions, or taking some other action than they would have from reading only quantitative research reports.

c. The detail in a case study helps readers compare the cases with their own situations.

d. The researcher typically reveals her personal perspective, so readers can compare their perspective to that of the researcher.

e. Case study research is well suited to the study of unusual or atypical phenomena.

f. Case study design is emergent and therefore flexible, so the researcher can more easily make changes while the research is in progress.

Disadvantages

a. Because case study research does not adhere to the sampling logic of quantitative research, it is more difficult to generalize the findings to other situations with assurance.

b. Ethical problems can arise if it proves difficult when reporting the case study to disguise the identity of the organization or individuals that were studied.

c. Case study research is highly labor intensive for the researcher.

d. Case study research demands a high level of verbal, analytic, and social skills from the researcher.

APPLICATION PROBLEMS

Problem 1

A researcher has obtained a grant to carry out a case study involving a multiple-case design to examine how policies about the education of migrant workers' children have changed over time. Describe the skills that the researcher will need to conduct this case study successfully.

<u>Sample Answer:</u>

 a. The researcher should have sufficient expertise, and the ability to present a professional identity and appearance, to interact with gatekeepers within the school hierarchy (e.g., state education officers in charge of migrant or bilingual education and administrators of schools with a large migrant population).

 b. The researcher should have sufficient familiarity with the needs and life patterns of migrant families to be comfortable and knowledgeable in collecting data from such families.

 c. The researcher should have sufficient time available to collect qualitative data through whatever data-collection methods are most appropriate, e.g., attending meetings and social events, analyzing historical documents that contain educational policy statements, and conducting interviews with school personnel and migrant children and adults.

 d. The researcher needs to have the skills for managing the project so that each case receives sufficient attention as well as for analyzing the data so that important similarities and differences between the cases are revealed.

 e. The researcher needs good verbal skills for interacting with participants in the field setting and for writing a case study report that brings this phenomenon alive for the readers.

Problem 2

The following narrative describes a graduate student's research proposal for a case study concerning leadership among students from different ethnic groups. List criticisms that an experienced qualitative researcher might make of the proposal.

"This study is concerned with the social structure of a fifth-grade class made up of students representing the following ethnic groups: 12 whites, 8 African-Americans, 4 Hispanics, 2 Asian-Americans, and 1 Native-American (Ute Indian). The research hypothesis is that there is no relationship between ethnicity and leadership status in the classroom. A random sample of 10 students will be selected and observed in class for a one-week period. An observation form has been designed for use in checking the number of leadership remarks made by each student."

Sample Answer:

a. Case study researchers usually ground their theoretical interpretations in the data rather than stating a definite hypothesis before collecting data.

b. A random sample is not likely to include representatives from each ethnic group. It would be preferable to select a purposeful sample, or to observe all the students.

c. Instead of using a structured observation form, the researcher probably would learn more by continuous recording (ideally on videotape) of what went on in the classroom. Then the researcher would be able to develop coding categories, if desired, and code and recode each data segment until she was confident that she had captured all significant instances of students' leadership behavior (nonverbal as well as verbal) and understood their meaning from an emic perspective.

d. A one-week observation period probably is too short to collect sufficient qualitative data.

Problem 3

Evaluate the strengths and weaknesses of the following proposal for a case study with the questions for evaluating a qualitative research report in Appendix G.

"The study will be carried out in an inner-city high school. It is aimed at studying teachers' interactions with one another and with students in as many school-related situations as possible, including faculty meetings, classes, and informal contacts in the cafeteria, teachers' lounge, on the playground, and in the halls. Two individuals who are employed half time as teachers in the school will serve as participant observers for one school year. Their role in the research will not be revealed until all data have been collected. Concurrent with their observations, two experienced researchers will conduct survey interviews with all teachers and a sample of students. Unstructured interviews also will be conducted at regular intervals with a group of key informants that includes teachers, students, and other school personnel."

Sample Answer:

a.   As part-time teachers at the school, the participant observers should have a good opportunity to obtain data on most teachers and many of the students. Because they have teaching responsibilities as well, they need some convenient method of recording the data so that it is available for later analysis. As participants, it would not be appropriate for them to audiotape or videotape interactions. They should agree on a note-taking method that provides detailed information and allows them to check inter-observer reliability.

b.   Freedom of access should be good in that the participant observers will have access to any meetings that they can legitimately attend in their role as teachers. Their access to other teachers' interactions with students, however (e.g., interactions during classes taught by other teachers), might be limited by the nature of the school organization

c.   Because observations will be made for an entire school year, the participant observers should have a good opportunity to sample the varied types of interaction situations in which they are interested. Again, they need some method to ensure that they record all the situations of interest, so they probably need a preplanned schedule for how they use their free time and where to locate themselves within the school during those times.

d.   It should be possible to collect both qualitative and quantitative data. It might be appropriate to focus the participant observers' observations and the key informant interviews on qualitative data. The two researchers could collect some quantitative data during the survey interviews (e.g., asking interviewees to rate the frequency of various types of interactions in which they engage).

e.   Triangulation can be achieved in this study by gathering information on the same topics using both the participant observers' field notes and the data from the interviews.

f.   Participant observers probably will need to use concealment, if not outright deception, to keep others unaware of their research activities. Collecting data about other teachers and staff without their knowledge raises ethical issues, and could create problems once their role is revealed. It probably would be better to tell school personnel that these two teachers will be making observations as part of the research, but to keep their research role as unobtrusive as possible.

TEACHING ACTIVITIES

Activity 1
Have students describe some of the phenomena having to do with education (in its broadest sense) that they find interesting. Work through several examples in which the class defines a research problem involving the phenomenon, a manageable focus for studying the phenomenon, a unit of analysis if appropriate, and the case or cases to be selected or sampled within that unit of analysis.

Activity 2

Select a research article reporting a simple educational case study and assign it as homework reading. In class have students describe the phenomenon, focus, unit of analysis if any, and the case or cases that the study involves. Ask students to use the concepts presented in the chapter to summarize the researcher's role in data collection and describe the approach to data analysis and reporting used in the case study.

Activity 3

Ask students to collect some qualitative data from or about an individual whom they know and are in a good position to interview or observe unobtrusively. If desired, provide a handout listing guidelines for doing the assignment, e.g., how specifically they should state the research problem, how they should select their case, how long or short the interview or observation period should be, and whether they should prepare a written report of their findings. Using the section topics in the chapter as a guide, have students report on their research experiences in class.

Activity 4

Invite a colleague to describe a completed case study in which the colleague participated as a researcher. Ask the presenter to focus on the particular problems that the case study involved and how they were handled, how the decision was made to end data collection, and the format or formats in which the case study was reported and why.

Note: The phrase in parentheses following the item number for both closed-form and open-form items, for example, 1. (obj. 3), refers to the textbook chapter objective to which the item is keyed.

CLOSED-FORM ITEMS

1. (obj. 1) Most qualitative research traditions
    a. have been used extensively in educational research.
    b. derive from the same academic discipline.
    c. are guided by similar epistemological assumptions.
    d. tend to borrow from one another over time.
Answer: d

2. (obj. 2) The tradition of cognitive psychology focuses on the study of
    a. lived experience from a positivist perspective.
    b. the world as it appears to individuals when engaged in unbiased reflection.
    c. the structures and processes involved in mental activity.
    d. cognitive phenomena that are common to all human beings.
Answer: c

3. (obj. 2) The researcher videotapes a teacher's lesson and then has the teacher view the tape and describe her thoughts and decisions that were occurring at the time. This example illustrates the method of inquiry in cognitive psychology called
    a. thinking aloud.
    b. stimulated recall.
    c. policy capturing.
    d. the repertory grid technique.
Answer: b

4. (obj. 3) A key criterion in selecting the participants for a phenomenological research study is that they
   a. are interested in expanding their understanding of the phenomenon being studied.
   b. agree to carry out contrived tasks and share their thinking as they perform the tasks.
   c. share the researcher's conceptions and values concerning the phenomenon being studied.
   d. are willing to be observed for an extended time period as they carry on their daily life.

Answer: a

5. (obj. 4) Phenomenography most differs from phenomenology in the former's
   a. interest in how reality appears to individuals.
   b. analysis of how individuals' differ in their conceptions of a given aspect of reality.
   c. interest in the objective nature of reality.
   d. use of indepth interviews as a method of collecting data.

Answer: b

6. (obj. 5) Most life history researchers
   a. are interested in how individuals interpret their life experiences.
   b. rely mainly on interviews and observations to collect data about individuals.
   c. use theories of cognitive development to make sense of individuals' interpretations of their life experiences.
   d. choose to write about their own life experiences.

Answer: a

7. (obj.'s 1-5) The following research traditions involve the investigation of lived experience. Match each tradition with the type of phenomenon that it investigates.
   ___ 1. Cognitive psychology.
   ___ 2. Life history.
   ___ 3. Phenomenography.
   ___ 4. Phenomenological research.
       a. Individuals' different conceptualizations of reality.
       b. Individuals' life experiences from their perspective.
       c. Mental structures and processes used by individuals in different situations.
       d. Reality as it appears to individuals.

Answer: 1=c, 2=b, 3=a, 4=d

8. The qualitative research tradition in which practitioners reflect on, and seek to improve the rationality and justice of, their work is called
    a. event structure analysis.
    b. emancipatory action research.
    c. symbolic interactionism.
    d. cultural studies.
Answer: b

9. (obj. 7) The research tradition that probably has most influenced the basic case study method as applied to educational research is
    a. cognitive psychology.
    b. life history.
    c. ethnography.
    d. symbolic interactionism.
Answer: c

10. (obj. 7) The assumed ability of individuals to shape the conditions of their lives is called ___ in qualitative research.
    a. cultural transmission
    b. cultural acquisition
    c. phenomenography
    d. agency
Answer: d

11. (obj. 8) A particular strength of ethnography is the researcher's
    a. holistic orientation to studying a culture or aspect of a culture.
    b. focus on the idiosyncrasies of various members of the culture.
    c. traditional concern for forming reciprocal relationships with those studied.
    d. preference for studying deviant or primitive cultures.
Answer: a

12. (obj. 9) An important difference between critical theory overall and the particular branch of critical theory called cultural studies is
    the former's concern for the
    a. investigation of the power relationships in a culture.
    b. emancipation of the members of cultural groups from systematized oppression.
    c. development of theories focused on large-scale social structure.
    d. understanding of the values and beliefs that underlie educational practice.
Answer: c

13. (obj. 9) The basic assumption of all critical theories is that
   a. all social inequalities need to be changed in order to make the world better place.
   b. no approach to seeking the truth is privileged over any other.
   c. cultural acquisition plays a minimal role in perpetuating forms of social and economic oppression.
   d. the members of oppressed groups are the best equipped to challenge the institutions that maintain their oppression.

Answer: a

14. (obj. 10) An approach that characterizes research and theory building in the cultural studies tradition is the
   a. analysis of the institutional system within which the researcher himself works.
   b. emphasis on long-term ethnographic investigation of subcultures within one's society.
   c. critique of the phenomena being studied, the methods used to study them, and the researcher's beliefs.
   d. use of language that reflects the everyday vocabulary of oppressed groups.

Answer: c

15. (obj. 11) Ethnomethodology differs from phenomenological research in the former's concern with
   a. the objective features of social reality.
   b. how groups develop intersubjective interpretations of reality.
   c. how social reality appears to individuals.
   d. the researcher's reflections on his own influence on the phenomena being studied.

Answer: b

16. (obj.'s 6-11) The following research traditions involve the investigation of society and culture. Match each tradition with the type of phenomenon that it investigates.

__ 1. Cultural studies.
__ 2. Emancipatory action research.
__ 3. Ethnography.
__ 4. Ethnomethodology.
__ 5. Event structure analysis.
__ 6. Symbolic interactionism.

    a. Characteristic features and patterns of a culture.
    b. Oppressive power relationships in a culture.
    c. Practitioners' self-reflective efforts to improve the rationality and justice of their work.
    d. The influence of social interactions on social structures and individuals' self-identity.
    e. The logical structures of social events.
    f. The rules that underlie everyday social interactions.

Answers: 1=b, 2=c, 3=a, 4=f, 5=e, 6=d

17. (obj. 12) A researcher studies the terms used by students and teachers to describe cheating in class in order to determine how individual members of the school culture conceptualize cheating behavior. This research is an example of

    a. the ethnography of communication.
    b. ethnographic content analysis.
    c. narrative analysis.
    d. ethnoscience.

Answer: d

18. (obj. 13) The hermeneutic circle in hermeneutics refers to

    a. the process of alternating between interpreting each part of a text and interpreting the whole.
    b. the flow of conversation between participants in a dialogue.
    c. the point at which participants' separate viewpoints recede into the background and a consensus emerges.
    d. the fact that both the author and the reader of a text are entangled in interpretive acts.

Answer: a

19. (obj. 14) In order to examine people's conformity to and deviation from the intended meaning of signs, a semioticist would be likely to
    a. analyze nonverbal sign systems rather than verbal sign systems
    b. combine fieldwork in a natural setting with a formal analysis of a sign system.
    c. focus her analysis on the denotative signs used by people.
    d. conduct a content analysis of the words used in people's dialogue.
Answer: b

20. (obj. 15) A principle that underlies structuralism as a research tradition is that
    a. the individual is the supreme definer of social reality.
    b. historical analysis is central to understanding a system as it exists at a given point in time.
    c. systems have little continuity because of the constant action of forces toward change.
    d. systems have self-regulating mechanisms that make them resistant to change.
Answer: d

21. (obj. 15) Poststructuralism is an approach to the study of systems based on the assumption that
    a. a system is best understood by focusing on the individual elements within it.
    b. the researcher's task is to discover the most objective interpretation of a literary work or text.
    c. texts include within themselves everything that is necessary for their interpretation.
    d. it is not possible to find any inherent meaning or value in a given system.
Answer: d

22. (obj.'s 12-15) The following research traditions involve the investigation of language and communication. Match each tradition with the type of phenomenon that it investigates.

___ 1. Ethnographic content analysis.
___ 2. Ethnography of communication.
___ 3. Ethnoscience.
___ 4. Hermeneutics.
___ 5. Narrative analysis.
___ 6. Semiotics.
___ 7. Structuralism.

    a. A culture's semantic systems.
    b. How members of a cultural group use speech in their social life.
    c. Organized representations and explanations of human experience.
    d. Signs and the meanings they convey.
    e. The content of documents in cultural perspective.
    f. The process by which individuals arrive at the meaning of a text.
    g. The systemic properties of language, text, and other phenomena.

Answers: 1=e, 2=b, 3=a, 4=f, 5=c, 6=d, 7=g

OPEN-FORM ITEMS

1. (obj. 1) Give two reasons why it is important for an educational researcher to become familiar with the major qualitative research traditions that have been used in educational research.

Answer (any 2 OK):

    a. Researchers are likely to encounter these traditions in their reviews of the research literature.

    b. Knowledge of the traditions will help a researcher formulate questions to guide a case study.

    c. Knowledge of the traditions will help researchers develop methods for collecting and analyzing research data in case studies.

    d. Knowledge of the traditions will suggest relevant theories to which researchers might connect their findings.

    e. A case study will have added meaning and significance if it is grounded within an established research tradition.

2. (obj. 1) Define the term *research tradition*.
Answer:
A research tradition is a group of scholars who agree among themselves on the nature of the universe they are examining, on legitimate questions and problems to study, and on legitimate techniques for seeking solution. The term refers also to the work of such scholars.

3. (obj. 1) Describe the three different types of phenomena on which different qualitative research traditions tend to focus.
Answer:
    a. Lived experience.
    b. Society and culture.
    c. Language and communication.

4. (obj. 2) Describe two methods that can be used to collect data in cognitive psychological research.
Answer (any 2 OK):
    a. Thinking aloud involves having an individual say everything that comes to mind as the individual carries out a task.
    b. Stimulated recall involves recording an episode on videotape or audiotape and having the main actor in the episode later view the recording and describe the thoughts and decisions that were occurring.
    c. Policy capturing involves asking research participants to rate written statements of hypothetical situations on Likert scales. A mathematical model then is constructed to describe the policies that are reflected in the responses.
    d. Journal keeping involves having research participants keep a written record of their plans or experiences. The journals are content-analyzed to generate descriptions and models of the processes of planning and reflection.
    e. The repertory grid technique involves having research participants sort cards with single words or statements on the basis of similarity and explain the basis for the sorts. Constructs are formulated based on the responses and arrayed in a grid format to show the relationships among the constructs.

5. (obj. 3) What is the difference between a textural description and a structural description of a phenomenon that is studied through phenomenological research?
Answer:
A textural description is an account of an individual's intuitive, prereflective perceptions of a phenomenon from every angle, whereas a structural description is an account of the cross-case regularities of thought, judgment, imagination, and recollection that underlie and give meaning to different individuals' experiences of a phenomenon.

6. (obj. 3) Describe one advantage of phenomenological research as a qualitative research method for use in education.
Answer (any 1 OK):
    a. It can be used to study a wide range of educational phenomena.
    b. The interview process used to collect phenomenological data is wide-ranging and therefore capable of detecting many aspects of experience that may prove to be important variables in subsequent quantitative studies.
    c. The procedures of phenomenological inquiry are relatively straightforward, so less training might be required to do a phenomenological study compared to a study based on some of the other research traditions.

7. (obj. 4) How would a phenomenographer's approach to studying teachers' views of the reasons for students' misbehavior in class differ from a phenomenological researcher's approach?
Answer:
A phenomenographer would study a group of teachers to develop a classification of their different conceptions of the reasons for students' misbehavior. A phenomenological researcher would be concerned with each teacher's total experience of student misbehavior, including his feelings, reflections, and associations with other life experiences.

8. (obj. 5) List two of the reporting formats in which a life history might be presented.
Answer (any 2 OK):
    a. Biography.
    b. Life story.
    c. Oral history.
    d. Case study.
    e. Autobiography.
    f. Memoir.

9. (obj. 6) What type of phenomena is the common focus of symbolic interactionism, event structure analysis, and emancipatory action research?
Answer:
These three research traditions focus on societal and cultural phenomena.

10. (obj. 7) Describe one of the key characteristics of ethnographic research.
Answer (any 1 OK):
   a. Its focus is on discovering cultural patterns in human behavior, that is, the communalities among individual human beings that are attributable to their culture.
   b.   Its focus is on the emic perspective of the members of the culture.
   c.   Its focus is on studying the natural settings in which culture is manifested, and studying all aspects of the setting.

11. (obj. 7) Describe one method that an ethnographic researcher uses to achieve the goal of looking at a cultural phenomenon from the perspective of an outsider and then seeking to understand the phenomenon from the perspective of insiders.
Answer (any 1 OK):
   a. The ethnographer can immerse herself in a culture that is far different from her own.
   b.   The ethnographer can study a subculture in her own community with which she is unfamiliar.
   c.   The ethnographer working in a familiar setting can take a different perspective from the one she normally uses, e.g., from a researcher perspective focused on theory rather than a teacher perspective focused on practice.

12. (obj. 8) Describe one strength and one weakness of ethnographic research.
Answer (any 1 from each set OK):
Strengths
a. It is particularly suited to investigating the complex phenomenon known as culture because of its holistic orientation.
b. It is able to identify the diverse elements of a culture and weave them into coherent patterns.
c. It enables the researcher to anticipate and interpret what goes on in a society or social group as appropriately as one of its members.
Weaknesses
a. It often is not clear whether a given ethnography subscribes to the goal of the natural sciences to develop natural laws or to the goal of the humanities to understand the unique and particular case.
b. Ethnographers impose their own order on cultural phenomena, which calls the validity of ethnographies into question.
c. Traditional ethnographies have not involved a reciprocal relationship with the members of the culture who were studied.

13. (obj. 9) What does cultural studies investigate, and what is its purpose?
Answer:
Cultural studies involves the investigation of power relationships in a culture, for the purpose of helping to emancipate members of the culture from the many forms of oppression that are perceived to operate within it.

14. (obj. 10) Describe one of the two main foci of cultural studies in education.
Answer (any 1 OK):
a. The study of educational programs and systems.
b. Theory-building.

15. (obj. 11) What is the purpose of the technique of breaching in an ethnomethodological study?
Answer: Breaching involves the occurrence of natural or contrived disruptions in people's normal routines. It is used to reveal the hidden work that people do to maintain the rules and routines by which their social environment normally operates, and thus to shed light on those rules and routines.

16. (obj. 12) Name and briefly describe one of the methods that can be used in narrative analysis.

Answer (any 1 OK):

a. Conversation analysis involves the study of the rules of speech acts between two or more people.

b. Sociolinguistics is the study of the effects of social characteristics such as age, socioeconomic status, and ethnicity on language use.

c. Narratology is the study of literary narratives.

d. Cognitive psychology is the study of the mental structures and processes used by individuals in different situations.

e. Ethnomethodology is the study of the rules that underlie everyday social interactions.

f. Event structure analysis is the study of the logical structures of social events.

17. (obj. 13) Why has hermeneutics had so much influence on the general approach of qualitative researchers?

Answer:

Interpretation of meanings is at the heart of hermeneutics. Interpretation of meanings also is a major focus of investigation in qualitative research. Therefore, qualitative researchers have looked to hermeneutic philosophers and researchers for insights into the interpretive process.

18. (obj. 14) Why would the research tradition of semiotics appear to have particular promise for educational researchers?

Answer:

Semiotics involves the study of sign systems, and many educational phenomena involve sign systems that are used to impart information and that thus affect what and how students learn.

19. (obj. 15) Explain the meaning of the structuralist principle, "the whole is greater than the sum of its parts" as it applies to the study of social groups.

Answer:

A social group is more than its individual members and how each interacts with the others. There is a sense of a group that exists independently of individual members and that influences the actions of each individual in the group.

20. (obj. 15) How does poststructuralism differ from structuralism in its assumptions about systems?

Answer:

Structuralism proposes to understand the inherent meaning of a system by the study of its elements, their relationships, and the overarching nature of the system itself. Poststructuralism, by contrast, argues that it is not possible to find any inherent meaning in a system but that all the only possibility is to examine the varied interpretations of a text, which are infinite.

APPLICATION PROBLEMS

Problem 1

Select a phenomenon of interest to you within the field of education, e.g., the effect of competitive athletics programs on students' experience of attending college. Describe one way in which you could study an aspect of that phenomenon through a tradition involving the investigation of (a) lived experience, (b) society and culture, and (c) language and communication.

Sample Answer:

The researcher could study students who are participants in an athletic program at a given university, e.g., the football team.

    a.   In an investigation of lived experience, the researcher could use the tradition of phenomenological research to have students reflect on how competitive athletics affects their experience of being students at the university.

    b.   In an investigation of society and culture, the researcher could use the tradition of cultural studies to examine how promising high school athletes with borderline achievement or from poor families are recruited with the promise of scholarships, tuition waivers, tutoring assistance, etc. to attend the university and participate in its athletic programs, and how athletic injuries alter students' present and future well being.

    c.   In an investigation of language and communication, the researcher could use the tradition of the ethnography of communication to study the language used by the coach and players during the half-time pep talk and how the language differs (e.g., in the use of metaphors involving battle and overcoming failure) depending on the score at half time.

Problem 2

Say that you are in the process of planning your master's or doctoral research study. You have decided first to select a research tradition that interests you and then to define a problem that can be studied by that tradition. Describe at least three of your personal characteristics (e.g., interests, abilities, and experience) that you might take into account in selecting the research tradition of greatest interest to you, and indicate some of the traditions that would appeal to you based on each of these characteristics.

Sample Answer:

    a. You might take your own educational background into account. For example, a student who majored in sociology as an undergraduate might prefer to base her research on a tradition involving the investigation of society and culture, whereas a linguistics major might wish to use a tradition involving the investigation of language and communication.

    b. You might consider whether you prefer a high level of structure when studying a problem or whether you prefer a low level of structure. If you like more structure, you might prefer ethnomethodology or event structure analysis, whereas if you prefer less structure you might want to base your study on symbolic interactionism or ethnography.

    c. You might consider whether you have a critical view of educational systems in our society or a more positive view. If you have a critical view, cultural studies or emancipatory action research may be well suited to serve as a foundation for your research study.

Problem 3

A teacher decides to carry out an ethnography involving the study of the school in which he works. Describe (a) one way in which the teacher could define the research problem to make the study more manageable to carry out within a reasonable time frame and (b) one way in which he could "make the familiar strange" in order to balance the emic and etic perspectives of the phenomenon he investigates.

Sample Answer:

    a. The teacher could make the study more manageable by limiting his focus to one aspect of the school phenomenon, e.g., the peer culture among students.

    b. He could make the familiar strange by studying a subculture in the school with which he is unfamiliar, which again is exemplified by focusing on the peer culture among students. Another way to make the familiar strange would be to step back from his teacher role and emphasize his researcher role when he thinks about what he is learning from the data he has collected.

TEACHING ACTIVITIES

Activity 1
Assign an educational research article to students having to do with a qualitative research tradition with which you have some familiarity. Have students work in groups to identify the phenomenon that the research involved, the data-collection method or methods used to study it, the methods used to analyze the data, whether they agree with the researcher's interpretations of the findings, and what they consider to be the strong and weak points of the study.

Activity 2
Have students identify a research problem of personal interest. Ask them to select two different qualitative research traditions they think would be useful in studying this problem and make a tentative list of the steps in a research study on the problem that are based on each of these two traditions. Have them compare the two lists and identify possible advantages and disadvantages in using one tradition versus the other.

Activity 3
Have students do a literature search to identify a research report involving one of the traditions covered in this chapter, read the report, and make a presentation in class in which they summarize the problem, the methods of study, and the findings of the research.

CHAPTER 16
HISTORICAL RESEARCH

Note: The phrase in parentheses following the item number for both closed-form and open-form items, for example, 1. (obj. 3), refers to the textbook chapter objective to which the item is keyed.

CLOSED-FORM ITEMS

1. (obj. 1) Unlike other types of social science researchers, historical researchers
   a. engage in causal inference.
   b. are concerned primarily with compiling facts.
   c. use subjective judgment to interpret events.
   d. discover rather than create data.
Answer: d

2. (obj. 1) An important goal of historical research is to
   a. test recent social science theories against historical data.
   b. interpret past events by using current concepts and perspectives.
   c. establish as many facts as possible about past events.
   d. gain an increased understanding of present-day phenomena by studying past events.
Answer: d

3. (obj. 1) Compared to historical research in the nineteenth century, contemporary historical research
   a. tends to be more factually complete.
   b. places more emphasis the interpretation of historical events.
   c. places greater reliance on archival records.
   d. relies more on secondary sources.
Answer: b

4. (obj. 2) Match each example below with the use of historical research it illustrates.
   __ 1.   A historian examines state department of education regulations from 1950 to 1990 for sexist content.
   __ 2.   A historian analyzes the textbooks used to teach reading in a particular school district during the last 75 years.
   __ 3.   A state education association newsletter presents a report card showing how various candidates seeking nomination to run for the U.S. presidency have voted on education-related bills.
   __ 4.   A researcher studies reports of research on the relationship between intelligence and socioeconomic status since the first intelligence test was developed.
      a.   Reviewing the literature in one's area of interest.
      b.   Collecting information concerning past educational practices.
      c.   Sensitizing educators to past practices that require reform.
      d.   Predicting future trends.

Answer: 1=c, 2=b, 3=d, 4=a

5. (obj. 3) Reading several historiographical works before undertaking a historical study particularly helps a historical researcher to
   a.   identify the most appropriate historical sources to obtain.
   b.   define the problem for the research study.
   c.   specify the steps and procedures to be used in the research.
   d.   avoid misinterpretations of historical data.

Answer: c

6. (obj. 4) Which of the following is *not* a typical topic for historical research?
   a.   Histories of specific individuals.
   b.   Relating past ideas or events that were not previously viewed as related.
   c.   Comparing learning outcomes from a new curriculum program with outcomes from a curriculum program that was used during the preceding era.
   d.   Revisionist reinterpretation of past events.

Answer: c

7. (obj. 4) Revisionist history refers to studies of
   a.   reform movements within various disciplines.
   b.   the historical causes of current social problems.
   c.   past events based on new interpretive frameworks.
   d.   utopian conceptions of education and other social institutions.

Answer: c

8. (obj. 5) A useful classification of historical documents is
    a. primary vs. secondary.
    b. published vs. unpublished.
    c. intentional vs. unpremeditated.
    d. all of the above.
Answer: d

9. (obj. 5) The four main types of historical sources are documents, quantitative records, relics, and
    a. repositories.
    b. oral records.
    c. instructional devices.
    d. computer software programs.
Answer: b

10. (obj. 6) In historical research, secondary sources are defined as those documents in which the
    a. description is written from an objective viewpoint.
    b. individual describing the event was not present at its occurrence.
    c. individual describing the event was a direct witness.
    d. historian reports events using her own interpretive framework.
Answer: b

11. (obj. 6) A researcher relies on sources published between 1910 and the present to investigate home schooling as practiced by pioneers who went West in the nineteenth century. This study illustrates the error of
    a. excessive use of secondary sources.
    b. failure to reconcile discrepant accounts of past events.
    c. studying an educational practice that cannot be viewed objectively because of current controversy about it.
    d. attempting to work on a broad and poorly defined problem.
Answer: a

12. (obj. 7) Recording information from a historical source usually
    a. requires reproduction of the entire document.
    b. requires computer technology.
    c. must be done by an official archivist.
    d. is affected by the copyright status of the source.
Answer: d

13. (obj. 8) Internal criticism of a historical source involves consideration of all of the following *except*
    a. the competence of the historical writer.
    b. whether the stated author actually wrote the document.
    c. possible indicators of the writer's bias, e.g., emotionally charged language.
    d. the accuracy of the facts presented in the document.
Answer: b

14. (obj. 8) Which of the following analyses can be of assistance in external criticism of a historical source?
    a. Analysis of the physical document, such as the paper used.
    b. Analysis of the author's biases.
    c. Analysis of discrepant accounts of a historical event.
    d. Analysis of the individual's personal stake in the events being described.
Answer: a

15. (obj. 8-9) Match each of the following procedures of historical research with the appropriate example of that procedure.
    ___ 1. Internal criticism of a historical document.
    ___ 2. External criticism of a historical document.
    ___ 3. Making a synthesis of data.
    ___ 4. Revisionist reinterpretation of past events.
    a. Collecting evidence to determine whether a historical source is a forgery.
    b. Judging whether the writer was competent to report on the events described in the source.
    c. Examining newly discovered historical documents to determine whether they reinforce existing interpretations of events.
    d. Writing a history of World War II that makes no mention of the Holocaust.
Answer: 1=b, 2=a, 3=c, 4=d

16. (obj. 9) Identifying forgeries, originals versus copies, and the date of origin of a historical document are all relevant to ___ of the document.
    a. internal criticism
    b. external criticism
    c. quantitative analysis
    d. historiographical analysis
Answer: b

17. (obj. 10) In historical research, an individual's public and private statements that give discrepant accounts of events are best viewed as
   a. two sources of data about the person making the statement.
   b. a sign of bias or prejudice.
   c. an example of antiquarianism.
   d. an example of the unreliability of observers' accounts.
Answer: a

18. (obj. 11) "History means interpretation" implies that
   a. there is no discernible objective reality in past events.
   b. all accounts and impressions of a past event are equally valid.
   c. historians rewrite the past in line with their own interests and concerns.
   d. current concepts rarely are useful for understanding earlier practices.
Answer: c

19. (obj. 12) The use of current concepts from other social science disciplines
   a. is a recent trend in historical research in education.
   b. rarely is useful for explaining past educational events.
   c. is an alternative to the traditional practice of external criticism in historical research in education.
   d. has helped check the movement toward revisionist history.
Answer: a

20. (obj. 12) Presentism is the practice of
   a. interpreting past events by using current concepts and perspectives.
   b. subordinating historical facts to the interpretive framework used to explain them.
   c. rejecting tradition in favor of change for its own sake.
   d. explaining current events in terms of the recent past rather than in terms of longterm historical trends.
Answer: a

21. (obj. 13) Historians generally believe that
   a. history repeats itself.
   b. ideology is the major causative agent in history.
   c. historical events are unique.
   d. the search for causes of past events is not an appropriate objective for historical research.
Answer: c

22. (obj. 13) Finding consistency in the historical accounts of different reporters assures a historian that she
   a. has made the correct causal interpretation of a past event.
   b. has studied the entire range of perspectives on the phenomenon of concern.
   c. can generalize the findings from examination of a relatively small sample of all the available primary sources.
   d. has obtained a representative sample of historical sources.
Answer: c

23. The methods of quantitative history have proved to be particularly useful for
   a. causal interpretation of past events.
   b. making broad generalizations about the past.
   c. external criticism of historical sources.
   d. measuring individuals' attitudes toward past events.
Answer: b

24. (obj. 14) A historical research dissertation includes these chapter titles: "School Choice, 1920-1940"; "School Choice, 1941-1960"; "School Choice, 1961-1980." This dissertation appears to be organized
   a. similarly to dissertations involving other types of educational research.
   b. consistent with a revisionist historical perspective.
   c. in relation to topics or themes.
   d. in chronological order.
Answer: d

25. (obj. 14) If a student uses concepts and descriptions with strong affective or value connotations in a historical research dissertation, the student should
   a. substantiate them by indicating the sources on which they are based.
   b. replace them with more moderate language in the final version of the dissertation.
   c. use direct quotes to convey each concept and description.
   d. summarize the student's personal experiences that underlie his choice of language.
Answer: a

OPEN-FORM ITEMS

1. (obj. 1) What is the main difference between contemporary and nineteenth-century historical research?
Answer:
Contemporary research emphasizes interpretation, whereas nineteenth-century research emphasized the compilation of as many objective facts as possible.

228

2. (obj. 2) State two purposes for studying the past.
Answer (any 2 OK):
   a. For its own sake, because one is interested in a particular historical period or event.
   b. To help us understand the past, in particular, to learn from past mistakes.
   c. To gain knowledge and insights for building on past research and practice.
   d. To provide a moral framework for understanding the present.
   e. To find evidence to support current proposals for social reform.
   f. To define and evaluate alternative future scenarios involving a particular educational phenomenon.

3. (obj. 3) The initial step in doing historical research is to define the problem or question to be investigated. Briefly describe three subsequent steps that are typical of the historical research process.
Answer:
   a. Search for sources of historical data..
   b. Read, summarize, and evaluate the historical sources.
   c. Report the pertinent data within an interpretive framework.

4. (obj. 4) Beach classified the problems and topics that can be addressed by historical research into five types, including current social issues such as home schooling and the growth of performance tests. Briefly describe and give an example of two other types of historical research problems.
Answer (any 2 OK):
   a. Histories of specific individuals, institutions, or movements. Example: the history of cooperative learning in U.S. schools.
   b. Exploration of relationships between ideas or events that previously appeared to be unrelated. Example: how the increased availability of personal computers has affected educators' conceptions of the teaching of writing.
   c. Efforts to synthesize old data collected by different historians or to merge old data with new historical facts. Example: using recent oral histories of teachers' lives to reexamine statements of educational policy earlier in this century.
   d. Reinterpretation of past events within new interpretive frameworks in order to sensitize educators to past practices that appear to have had unjust aims and effects but that have continued into the present and thus require reform. Example: how educational innovation in mid-nineteenth century New England schools served to thwart democratic aspirations.

5. (obj. 5) List two of the main types of primary sources used in historical research, and give an example of each.

Answer (any 2 OK):

   a.   Written documents or records. Example: the diary of someone who was part of the Lewis and Clark expedition to Oregon.

   b.   Quantitative records. Example: school records of student attendance, test scores, or program budgets.

   c.   Oral records. Example: audiotapes of oral interviews with people who were students when the U.S. instituted busing as a strategy for integrating the public schools.

d. Relics. Example: a collection of different computers used in the schools during the last 25 years.

6. (obj. 6) Describe the three main types of historical sources used by a historical researcher and the purpose of each.

Answer:

   a.   Preliminary sources are indexes that list secondary and primary sources relevant to historical research generally or to a particular historical period or topic. They are used to identify the appropriate secondary and primary sources to use in research on a specific historical problem.

   b.   Secondary sources are documents in which an individual who was not present at an event gives an account of the event. They are used to summarize information about a historical event that usually has been gained from numerous primary sources and perhaps from other secondary sources as well.

   c.   Primary sources are records (documents, quantitative records, oral records, or relics) that were generated by people who personally witnessed or participated in the historical events of interest. They provide the ultimate basis for the facts that historians present in historical research studies.

7. (obj. 7) A researcher has identified several primary sources that appear ideal for exploring her research topic. Describe two issues with which the researcher must deal before she is able to collect and record pertinent information from these sources.

Answer:

   a.   The researcher must determine whether the sources that she wishes to use will be made accessible to her, and under what conditions.

   b.   The researcher must find out whether information in the materials can be copied and reproduced in the dissertation.

8. (obj. 8) In examining a document, the historical researcher uses external criticism. Explain what this involves.
Answer:
External criticism deals with the evaluation of the authenticity of the source. It involves addressing such questions as, Is it genuine? Is it the original copy? When, where, and by whom was it written?

9. (obj. 9). In examining a document, the historical researcher uses internal criticism. Explain what this involves.
Answer:
Internal criticism deals with the evaluation of the credibility of the information contained in the document. It involves addressing such questions as, Is it probable that people would act in the way described by the writer? Is it physically possible for the events to have occurred as described? Do the quantitative data presented appear to be correct? The researcher needs to consider the writer's expertise, honesty, and role in the events, including possible conflicts of interest.

10. (obj. 10) Bias in a historical account involves the writer or informant having a strong set to perceive events in such a way that certain types of facts habitually are overlooked, distorted, or falsified. Briefly describe two common causes of such bias.
Answer (any 2 OK):
    a.   People often exaggerate their own roles in important events.
    b.   The truth often is elaborated upon or colored in order to make the account more interesting.
    c.   The person's position leads him to give socially acceptable rather than truthful information, e.g., a person in a political or administrative role.
    d.   The individual's past experience with the phenomenon is such that he has reason to distrust the motives and actions of others.

11. (obj. 11) What is presentism, and how can it affect historical research?
Answer:
Presentism is the tendency of the historian to interpret past events using concepts and perspectives that originated after the events occurred. For example, terms such as *accountability* do not mean the same thing today as they did 30 years ago. The use of such a concept in interpreting past events can create misunderstanding of those events.

12. (obj. 12) Name one benefit and one possible drawback of a historical researcher's use of particular concepts to interpret historical data.

Answer (any 1 from each set OK):

Benefits

a. Concepts allow the researcher to show the relationship between many historical phenomena that otherwise might be seen as separate or insignificant.

b. Concepts allow the researcher to explore possible causal interpretations of historical events that have not previously been considered.

Drawbacks

a. The way in which a concept is defined places limits on what the historian chooses to explore.

b. If a concept meant something different at the time the historical event occurred than it does now, its use can create misunderstanding of the meaning of the event.

13. (obj. 13) Explain why it is difficult for historians to attribute a historical event to a single cause.

Answer:

A given event has many antecedents that could have influenced the event. Various plausible interpretations can be posed for any event, each of which explains some of the evidence, leaves other evidence unexplained, and suggests new questions to ask. Many of the possible causes may not even have been discovered. Thus it is difficult to justify attributing the event to a single cause.

14. (obj. 13) Briefly describe one problem faced by historians in generalizing from their findings.

Answer (any 1 OK):

a. Available sources almost always constitute a nonrepresentative sample of all the relevant records that once existed related to a given event.

b. In studying individuals a similar problem arises, in that the available records for one point in time may not accurately represent the individual's opinion or behavior at a different time.

15. (obj. 14) Describe three approaches to organizing the research findings in a historical research dissertation and give an example of each.

a. Present the historical facts in chronological order. Example: Each chapter in a dissertation about the educator Horace Mann covers a discrete period in his life, i.e., childhood, adolescence, young adulthood, and maturing years.

b. Present the historical facts according to topics or themes. Example: In a study of the growth of private schooling in the U.S., each chapter of the dissertation covers one of the major presumed causes for this growth, i.e., religious movements, reduced funding of public education, parental concerns about school violence, and trends in student achievement.

c. Combine the chronological and thematic approaches. Example: Each chapter in a study of the development of private tutoring services in the U.S. is thematic, covering a particular type of service (i.e., test preparation services, tutoring services focused on remediation, and tutoring services focused on fostering giftedness or creativity); and the internal organization of the chapter is chronological (i.e., pre-1950, 1950-1979, 1980-1989, and 1990 to the present).

APPLICATION PROBLEMS

Problem 1
A researcher is carrying out historical research about the impact of computers on instruction in the public schools between 1970 and 1990. Although the study primarily id qualitative in design, name one type of quantitative information that the researcher might wish to report concerning this research problem.
Sample Answer:
The researcher might want to report the number and proportion of students of various types who received computer instruction or otherwise had access to computers, for example, by grade, gender, or ability level.

Problem 2
Suppose you are doing a study about policies for the allocation of funds to teacher salaries, books and other instructional materials, plant maintenance and operation, and administrative costs in three rural elementary schools during the period 1900 to 1930. One of your main sources for this study are the account books for each school, in which the principals listed by date each expenditure as it occurred and entered a brief description. In studying this source, how would you record the information needed for your data analysis?
Sample Answer:
A document summary form (see chapter 14) can be prepared for recording the specific types of information needed for your research. You should note on each copy of the form the source of the information (e.g., Washington Elementary School account book, school year 1900-1901). For each entry you could list the date, the dollar amount, and the category that each entry reflects (teacher salary, books, etc.). You could also record anything about the entry worthy of special note (e.g., payment of a teacher in goods rather than money). When you have prepared all the forms, you could sort them in different ways to answer specific questions, such as, How similar were the spending patterns of the different principals? What trends occurred in expenditures for educational materials from 1900 to 1930?

Problem 3
Suppose that you are doing a historical study on the teaching of pseudosciences in U.S. public schools during the period 1870-99. You find the following article in the April 15, 1891, issue of the *Sonoma Farmer*, a rural weekly newspaper published in California:

Wonders of the Science of Phrenology

Local citizens attending the County Fair this week are being amazed by Professor Horatio Horton, a leading practitioner of the science of Phrenology. Professor Horton can make infallible analyses of the character and personality of any man or woman by feeling the bumps on the individual's head. Most persons overheard by your reporter agreed that the Professor's analyses of people out of the audience were uncanny.

After the performance your reporter interviewed the Professor in his dressing room and learned that he is a leader in the movement to teach Phrenology in the public schools. The Professor himself has taught the science to thousands of students in colleges and high schools throughout most of the civilized nations of the world. Phrenology is now a required subject in the secondary schools of France, Italy and several other European countries. Students in these countries usually devote a year to the study of this valuable science.

The Professor strongly recommends that local citizens apply pressure to county officials to bring about inclusion of Phrenology in the local curriculum. He is available to give teachers a short course in the science and has also written several books and pamphlets that would be useful to students. Your reporter feels that adequate training in Phrenology should be provided in our schools as soon as possible. After all, your children are entitled to a modern education.

Conduct an internal criticism of this source by listing several reasons why the accuracy of the information in the article can be questioned.
Sample Answer:
    a. The reporter had not himself witnessed the teaching of phrenology referred to by the professor.
    b. The professor had a financial interest in making phrenology appear important.
    c. The reporter did not interview a purposeful sample of audience members but simply reported what he overheard.
    d. The professor appears to have exaggerated his expertise to impress the reporter.

Problem 4
A historian plans a research study on how early twentieth-century school officials and psychologists influenced each other with respect to the advocacy of intelligence testing.
a. What concepts does the historian need to define in doing this research, and why?
b. List several factors that will affect the generalizability of the historian's findings.
Sample Answer:
    a. *School official, psychologist, intelligence test*, and *early nineteenth-century* need to be defined because these concepts identify the range of phenomena to be included in the historical search.
    b. The number of years in the early twentieth century for which historical sources will be obtained; the range of psychologists and school officials whose views will be studied; the geographical locales (e.g., the entire U.S., individual states, and/or European countries) for which historical sources will be sought.

TEACHING ACTIVITIES

Activity 1
Locate a published account of a historical event that is relevant to education and that generated considerable controversy (e.g., a newspaper story about the first black student's entry to the University of Alabama during George Wallace's governorship of Alabama). Have students determine whether the source is a primary or secondary source, and ask them to carry out an internal criticism of the source.

Activity 2
Identify a researcher in your area who has carried out a historical research study relevant to education, and invite this person to be a guest presenter. Ask the researcher to describe why he carried out the study, any problems that arose in collecting and analyzing the data, the findings, and what he sees as the value of the research for present-day understanding of educational issues.

Activity 3
Identify a research article that describes a historical study in education. Have the students read the study as a homework assignment and then discuss in class the study's strengths and weaknesses. You might want to indicate the particular aspects of the study to which they should pay attention, e.g., the statement of the research problem, the quality of the sources used, and the appropriateness of the researcher's interpretations.

CHAPTER 17
EVALUATION RESEARCH

Note: The phrase in parentheses following the item number for both closed-form and open-form items, for example, 1. (obj. 3), refers to the textbook chapter objective to which the item is keyed.

CLOSED-FORM ITEMS

1. (obj. 1) Match each of the following examples of educational evaluation with the purpose for conducting an evaluation that it illustrates.

___ 1.   The developer of an innovative approach to teaching English to migrant children is asked for documentation of the success rates with this approach.

___ 2.   A high school principal asks an evaluator to collect data on the costs and benefits of the school's efforts to reduce student dropout.

___ 3.   Opponents of site-based management cite negative evaluations of this approach in a public hearing.

___ 4.   A researcher collects data to prepare a position paper on the costs, benefits, and problems of various means to promote adult literacy.

   a.   A guide to policy decisions in education.
   b.   A basis for advocacy for political action.
   c.   A component of the management of educational programs.
   d.   Use of research to design new programs meeting specified criteria of effectiveness.

Answer: 1=d, 2=c, 3=b, 4=a

2. (obj. 2) Evaluation research differs most from other types of educational research in its emphasis on
   a.   producing generalizable findings.
   b.   demonstrating statistically significant differences or relationships between variables.
   c.   yielding data concerning the value of educational phenomena.
   d.   obtaining the opinions of individuals about educational phenomena.

Answer: c

3. (obj. 3) An outside evaluator is hired to evaluate a school program that has special funding. A teacher tells him that he actually was brought in to collect data to justify the principal's plan to reassign several staff members. The evaluator's most appropriate action in this situation is to
   a. interview a variety of key individuals in the field setting to explore further the basis for the evaluation request.
   b. ask the teacher to provide evidence to support her claim.
   c. terminate the evaluation effort in the interests of ethical principles.
   d. ask the principal to reconfirm the previously stated purpose of the evaluation.

Answer: a

4. (obj. 4) The outcome of program delineation is
   a. a decision about which of the components of the program should be included in the evaluation.
   b. the selection of the specific model of evaluation to be used to evaluate the program.
   c. the determination of the effectiveness of the program that is evaluated.
   d. an identification of the most important characteristics of the program that is to be evaluated.

Answer: d

5. (obj. 4) An example of a program resource is the
   a. set of criteria used to hire staff for the program.
   b. objectives that program staff are committed to achieve.
   c. observed benefits of the program.
   d. staff needed to implement the program.

Answer: d

6. (obj. 4) Match each question with the component of an educational program that needs to be evaluated to answer it.
   ___ 1. How will students have changed following completion of the program?
   ___ 2. What are the obvious and hidden costs of the program?
   ___ 3. To what extent did teachers actually use the techniques recommended in the program?
   ___ 4. Did the principal's supervision of the teachers help them improve their use of program techniques?
   a. Program goals
   b. Program resources
   c. Program procedures
   d. Program management

Answer: 1=a, 2=b, 3=c, 4=d

7. (obj. 5) Gathering a comprehensive list of evaluation questions from all stakeholders is the ___ phase in selecting questions for an evaluation study.
   a. program delineation
   b. divergent
   c. goal definition
   d. convergent
Answer: b

8. (obj. 6) An important question to consider in creating a design for a program evaluation is,
   a. Which stakeholders should conduct the evaluation?
   b. How can the evaluation be conducted so as not to incur any costs?
   c. Can an outside evaluator be found who has a major stake in the program?
   d. How much internal and external validity can be built into the research design?
Answer: d

9. (obj. 7) Probably the most common type of quantitative research design used in evaluation studies is ___ research designs.
   a. correlational
   b. single-case
   c. experimental
   d. causal-comparative
Answer: c

10. (obj. 8) The report of an evaluation study typically differs from the report of a research study in that the former
   a. is simpler, because stakeholders only want the "bottom line."
   b. is prepared in different forms for different stakeholder groups.
   c. contains a more extensive review of the literature.
   d. places more emphasis on the generalizability of the findings.
Answer: b

11. (obj. 8) The *Standards for Evaluations of Educational Programs, Projects, and Materials* were developed to
   a. disseminate information about the exemplary quality of the standards currently used in evaluation research.
   b. reflect the varied political orientations of individuals working in the field of evaluation.
   c. assemble into one source several sets of standards that various research and educational organizations had thoroughly tested in the field.
   d. improve the professionalism of educational evaluation.
Answer: d

12. (obj. 8) The main focus of the *Standards for Evaluations of Educational Programs, Projects, and Materials* is
   a. optimizing the instrumental use of evaluation research.
   b. selecting the best strategy for assessment of educational personnel.
   c. assessing the feasibility of including an evaluation component in a program design.
   d. comparing individuals' test performance with the appropriate norms.
Answer: a

13. (obj. 9) Evaluation research as a special application of educational research can be traced back most clearly to
   a. the growing interest in qualitative research.
   b. research and development (R&D) in industry and medicine.
   c. the need for public funds to support compulsory education.
   d. the individual intelligence testing movement.
Answer: d

14. (obj. 9) Goal-free evaluation
   a. helps alert developers to adverse effects of the program.
   b. typically is carried out in the early stages of program development.
   c. involves collecting only data that are unrelated to the program's stated goals.
   d. is a collaborative effort between the evaluator and key stakeholders.
Answer: a

15. (obj. 9) Goal-free evaluation differs from other approaches to evaluation mainly in that it
   a. requires the evaluator to be uninformed of the intended goals of the program.
   b. requires unique statistical techniques.
   c. must be used to evaluate programs in the formative stage.
   d. is concerned primarily with negative program effects.
Answer: a

16. (obj. 9) The main rationale for the development of objectives-based evaluation was that
   a. information about individual differences in student aptitude is needed for selection decisions.
   b. students might perform poorly in school not because of a lack of innate ability but because of weaknesses in the curriculum.
   c. the merit of an educational program must be assessed in relation to the values and beliefs of different stakeholders.
   d. it is not possible to specify the most desired instructional outcomes in behavioral terms.
Answer: b

17. (obj. 9) The goal of a college education for all citizens who desire one is an example of a need stated as
   a. an expectation.
   b. a norm.
   c. a minimum.
   d. an ideal.

Answer: d

18. (obj. 9) Match each example of evaluation listed below with the type of evaluation in the CIPP model that it illustrates.
   ___ 1. Recruitment programs should be implemented for doctoral students who have the desired characteristics to become special education faculty members.
   ___ 2. The recruitment program has succeeded in attracting more Hispanic graduate students in special education, but the proportion of African-American students recruited has not changed.
   ___ 3. Not enough special education students are receiving doctorates to fill available faculty positions in special education.
   ___ 4. Attendance at recruitment program meetings designed to attract more minority students into special education revealed that a lower proportion of African-Americans and Hispanics attend the programs than their representation in the general graduate student body at this university.
   a. Context evaluation
   b. Input evaluation
   c. Process evaluation
   d. Product evaluation

Answer: 1=b, 2=d, 3=a, 4=c

19. (obj. 9) Match each of the procedures below with the type of educational evaluation that uses this procedure.
    ___ 1. The degree of congruence between program standards and actual program performance is determined .
    ___ 2. The relationship between program benefits and the resources needed to achieve those benefits is calculated.
    ___ 3. Data are collected about present needs, required resources and strategies, program operation, and goal achievement.
    ___ 4. Evaluators conduct research to discover the actual effects of the program in operation.
        a. Goal-free evaluation.
        b. Context-Input-Process-Product evaluation.
        c. Needs assessment.
        d. Cost analysis.
Answer: 1=c, 2=d, 3=b, 4=a

20. (obj.'s 9-10) Responsive evaluation models and objectives-based evaluation models differ on several important characteristics. Place an R in front of the characteristics of responsive evaluation and an 0 in front of the characteristics of objectives-based evaluation in the following list.
    ___ a. Uses a formal rather than an informal approach.
    ___ b. Focuses on identifying concerns and issues.
    ___ c. Is modeled after the procedures of experimental psychology.
    ___ d. Employs careful preplanning of the evaluation design.
    ___ e. Involves purposeful sampling of stakeholders.
Answer: a=O, b=R, c=O, d=O, e=R

21. (obj. 10) Which of the following is a characteristic of responsive evaluation?
    a. It makes extensive use of subjective inquiry.
    b. It focuses on objective response patterns.
    c. It refers to psychological theories of development.
    d. A research design first is developed and the evaluation responds to the demands of that design.
Answer: a

22. (obj. 10) A desirable requirement for a graduate student wishing to use responsive evaluation as a model for an evaluation study for a dissertation is that the student should
    a. be experienced in carrying out a variety of research designs.
    b. work with an experienced team of evaluators on a joint project.
    c. study a stratified sample of stakeholders.
    d. be a stakeholder in the program to be evaluated.
Answer: b

23. (obj. 10) Which of these evaluation models involves independent development of pro and con arguments concerning program-related issues?
    a. The Context-Input-Process-Product model.
    b. Discrepancy evaluation.
    c. Adversary evaluation.
    d. Goal-free evaluation.
Answer: c

24. (obj. 10) An important difference between adversary evaluation and judicial evaluation is that the former
    a. involves a public hearing in which presenters present cases for or against a particular position.
    b. is based on the use of legal procedures to review program characteristics.
    c. involves a debate between two evaluation teams, with victory or persuasion as the desired outcome.
    d. has been widely used in educational research.
Answer: c

25. (obj. 10) Unlike other qualitative models of evaluation, educational connoisseurship and criticism is unique in that
    a. the questions that motivate the evaluation are set by the evaluator alone.
    b. it combines both qualitative and quantitative research methods.
    c. the evaluative orientation toward the phenomena being studied is based on critical theory.
    d. it is based largely on the research tradition of cognitive anthropology.
Answer: a

26. (obj. 11) A decision by an educational research and development (R&D) specialist to abort further development of an educational program would most likely be made at the ___ stage of the R&D cycle.
    a. instructional analysis
    b. formative evaluation
    c. instructional revision
    d. summative evaluation
Answer: b

27. (obj. 11) Formative evaluation
    a. involves collecting data about an educational program while it is still under development in order to improve it.
    b. enables the researcher to generalize the findings to other programs and samples.
    c. involves testing research hypotheses about a program prior to submitting it to summative evaluation.
    d. is conducted by using primarily quantitative research methods.
Answer: a

28. (obj. 11) The three-level process of formative evaluation described in the text
    a. corresponds closely to the evaluation procedures used by major textbook publishers.
    b. moves progressively from a focus on qualitative methods to a focus on quantitative methods of evaluation.
    c. moves progressively from a focus on quantitative methods to a focus on qualitative methods of evaluation.
    d. involves a review of the program by stakeholders at each stage.
Answer: b

29. (obj. 11) In contrast to formative evaluation, summative evaluation
    a. involves a critical review of each program component by key stakeholders.
    b. is carried out by the evaluator working alone.
    c. is considered an integral part of the instructional design process.
    d. is likely to involve quantitative research methods.
Answer: d

30. (obj. 11) An important purpose of summative evaluation is to
    a. help developers determine what the goals of a program should be.
    b. determine how successful the program is under normal operating conditions.
    c. discover the goals of a program by observing the program while it is being developed.
    d. identify unintended outcomes for which the program has application.
Answer: b

31. (obj. 11) The main purpose of the National Diffusion Network (NDN) is to
    a. identify promising but as yet untested programs that are suitable for dissemination.
    b. serve as a clearinghouse on evaluation methodology and reports of meta-evaluations.
    c. distribute information about educational programs that have been found to be successful in summative evaluations.
    d. provide a preliminary source that indexes published summative evaluations.
Answer: c

32. (obj. 12) A common criticism of behavioral objectives is that they
    a. omit the situational context in which the behavior is to be performed.
    b. do not give stakeholders an adequate sense of what those who succeed as a result of the program will be able to do.
    c. do not provide much help in designing test items to evaluate program effectiveness.
    d. reduce education to a matter of teaching only that which is easily measured.
Answer: d

33. (obj. 12) Behavioral objectives are particularly helpful in
    a. determining the level of resources needed to develop an instructional program.
    b. determining the causes of students' failure to learn from an instructional program.
    c. designing test items to assess students' capabilities before and after experiencing an instructional program.
    d. one-on one testing of hypotheses derived from instructional design theory.
Answer: c

34. (obj. 13) A good way for a graduate student to design an educational research and development project to make it more manageable to conduct is to
    a. serve as both the developer and the evaluator for the project.
    b. compare the effectiveness of two alternate versions of the developed program.
    c. end the dissertation study after the preliminary field test stage.
    d. use only qualitative methods of evaluation.
Answer: c

OPEN-FORM ITEMS

1. (obj. 1) Describe two purposes for which educational evaluation studies are carried out.
Answer (any 2 OK):
    a. To determine the worth or merit of particular educational methods, materials, programs, organizations, or individuals.
    b. To provide information needed to guide educational policy making.
    c. To provide a basis to support or oppose particular political decisions.
    d. To assist in the management of educational programs.

2. (obj. 2) Briefly state one of the differences between educational evaluation and educational research.
Answer (any 1 OK):

    a. Evaluation usually is designed to aid a local decision, whereas research is concerned with producing knowledge.

    b. Evaluation usually is less generalizable, because it deals with a specific purpose or a limited question.

    c. Evaluation produces judgments of value, whereas research produces descriptive or theoretical knowledge.

3. (obj. 3) If evaluators are asked to conduct an evaluation, what procedure should they use to clarify the reasons for doing the evaluation?
Answer:
The usual procedure is to interview a variety of key individuals involved in the program to be evaluated in order to obtain an overall picture of the reasons, including any covert or unethical reasons, that an evaluation is desired.

4. (obj. 3)

    a. Define the term *stakeholder* as used in evaluation research.

    b. What are two reasons why stakeholders need to be identified as part of an evaluation study?
Answer:

    a. A stakeholder is anyone involved in the program being evaluated and/or anyone who may be affected by the results.

    b. Reasons for Identifying Stakeholders

        (1) Stakeholders can help the evaluator clarify the reasons for doing the evaluation; the questions that should guide the evaluation; and the best way to design the research, interpret the findings, and report the results.

        (2) If some stakeholders are ignored, they can sabotage the evaluation or try to discredit the results.

5. (obj. 4) List two of the procedures that should be followed in determining which aspects of the overall program should be evaluated.
Answer (any 2 OK):

    a. Program delineation, i.e., describing the significant characteristics or components of the program to be evaluated.

    b. Deciding what program characteristics or components will be evaluated.

    c. Specifying the program goals.

    d. Identifying program resources.

    e. Identifying program procedures.

    f. Describing the program's management system.

6. (obj. 5) What is the difference between the divergent phase and the convergent phase in selecting questions for an evaluation study?
Answer:
In the divergent phase, the evaluator gathers a comprehensive list of questions from all stakeholders and interested parties, whereas in the convergent phase the evaluator reduces the list to a manageable set of the most important questions.

7. (obj. 6) Briefly describe two of the questions that should be considered in developing an evaluation design.
Answer (any 2 OK):
    a. Should the evaluation be qualitatively or quantitatively oriented?
    b. Should an internal or external evaluator conduct the evaluation?
    c. How much internal and external validity should be built into the design?
    d. How can potentially negative effects of the evaluation be minimized?
    e. Can the evaluation be completed in the time available?

8. (obj. 6) What is one negative effect that can occur from the evaluation of an educational program?
Answer (any 1 OK):
    a. Personnel working in the program may resent the evaluator or feel threatened by the evaluation.
    b. A good program can be destroyed by a poor evaluation.
    c. Evaluation activities use resources that thus are not directly available to enhance the program.

9. (obj. 7) *The Standards for Evaluations of Educational Programs, Projects, and Materials* developed four major criteria for good evaluation studies: utility, feasibility, propriety, and accuracy. Describe one specific standard for each of these broad criteria.
Answer:
(Note: See the list of Standards on pp. 692-694 in the textbook; any one item from each part of the list is OK.)

10. (obj. 8) (a) What is a meta-evaluation, (b) what does a meta-evaluation include, and (c) is it part of evaluation research, other types of educational research, or both?
Answer:
    a. A meta-evaluation is an evaluation of an evaluation or a research study.
    b. It typically includes a discussion of the limitations and weaknesses in a study that could affect the validity of the results.
    c. Meta-evaluation is necessary in both research and evaluation studies.

11. (obj. 9) What is the main difference between the evaluation of individuals and objectives-based evaluation?
Answer:
The evaluation of individuals involves evaluating the individual against a standard and the study of individual differences, whereas objectives-based evaluation involves evaluating a program in terms of its success in promoting desired program objectives in program users.

12. (obj. 9) Name the three components of a behavioral objective.
Answer:
    a. A statement of the program objective as an observable, behavioral outcome.
    b. Criteria for judging successful performance of the behavior.
    c. The situational context (or "givens") within which the behavior is to be evaluated.

13. (obj. 9) Name two problems with objectives-based evaluation.
Answer (any 2 OK):
    a. Critics argue that they reduce education to a matter of teaching only that which can be stated and measured in the language of behavioral objectives.
    b. Bias can be introduced in selecting the particular objectives to measure.
    c. This approach does not offer much guidance if one wishes to understand why particular objectives are considered worthwhile or why certain stakeholders agree or disagree about the worth of certain objectives.
    d. The politics of evaluation is not given much attention in this approach.
    e. The evaluation process itself might hamper the very performance that is being assessed.

14. (obj. 9) What is meant by goal-free evaluation?
Answer:
Evaluation in which the evaluator does not know, or ignores, the goals of the program being evaluated. Thus, the evaluator is more likely to investigate both intended and unintended outcomes of the program.

15. (obj. 9) State one problem that can arise in doing a needs assessment.
Answer (any 1 OK):
    a. Unless the concept of need is defined the same way by everyone involved in the needs assessment, confusion or disagreement may arise.
    b. Many needs assessments do not make clear how urgent or optional are the desired states that are being determined.
    c. The values that underlie various needs often are not clearly articulated.
    d. Important individual differences in stated needs might be obscured by traditional methods of reporting group trends in a needs assessment.

16. (obj. 9) Briefly describe the four types of educational evaluation that are incorporated in the CIPP evaluation model.
Answer:

a. *Context evaluation*: identification of the problems and needs in a specific educational setting and development of program objectives that will alleviate the needs.

b. *Input evaluation*: identification of the resources and strategies needed to achieve the program objectives.

c. *Process evaluation*: design of an evaluation system and collection of day-to-day evaluation data as the program is put into operation (similar to formative evaluation).

d. *Product evaluation*: determination of the extent to which the program goals have been achieved (similar to summative evaluation).

17. (obj. 9) What is the main purpose of conducting a formative evaluation of an educational program?
Answer:
To obtain information that can be used to revise or modify the program to make it more effective.

18. (obj. 10) What is the main way in which qualitative approaches to evaluation differ from quantitative approaches?
Answer:
Qualitative approaches to evaluation are not based on the assumption that objective criteria exist for judging the worth of an educational program. Instead they assume that worth depends on the values and perspectives of whoever does the judging.

19. (obj. 10) Describe the four stages of adversary evaluation.
Answer:

a. Generating a broad range of issues concerning the program by surveying various stakeholders.

b. Reducing the issues to a manageable number.

c. Forming two opposing evaluation teams, one of which prepares an argument in favor of the program on each issue and the other of which prepares an argument opposed to the program on each issue.

d. Conducting prehearing sessions and a formal hearing in which the adversarial teams present their cases before individuals who must make a decision about the program.

20. (obj. 10) Describe one of the shortcomings of adversary evaluation.
Answer (any 1 OK):

    a. The results can be biased if one of the evaluation teams is more skilled in argumentation than the other.

    b. By its nature, it promotes a combative "innocent versus guilty" approach to program evaluation and thus may contribute to alienation among different types of stakeholders.

    c. It requires a great deal of time and a large number of people, and thus is expensive.

21. (obj. 10) In the qualitative evaluation model called educational connoisseurship and criticism, describe what connoisseurship and what criticism each involve.
Answer:
Educational connoisseurship involves appreciating (in the sense of becoming aware of) the qualities of an educational program and their meaning. Educational criticism involves describing and evaluating that which has been appreciated.

22. (obj. 11)

    a. Describe the role that evaluation plays in educational research and development.

    b. Describe the specific purpose of (1) formative evaluation and (2) summative evaluation.
Answer:

    a. After a program has been developed, it undergoes a progressively more stringent series of field testing and revision in which its effectiveness is evaluated in relation to whether learners exposed to the program can achieve its prespecified performance objectives.

    b. (1) Formative evaluation is carried out by the program developers while the program is still under development in order to improve its effectiveness.

       (2) Summative evaluation is carried out by others after the program has completed development in order to determine how worthwhile the program is, especially in comparison with other alternatives.

23. (obj. 11) Give two reasons why an educational program needs to be tested in a field setting that is similar to the context in which it ultimately will be used before it is released for dissemination.
Answer:

    a. The external validity of the research findings for the program will be higher in a field setting, that is, one can generalize the results more safely to other, similar settings.

    b. Often problems will occur in the field that would not occur in more controlled research situations. Thus a test in the field is necessary to provide valid data about the program's effectiveness.

24. (obj. 12) State one benefit of specifying performance objectives in developing an educational program.

Answer (any 1 OK):

a. Performance objectives provide a way to communicate clearly to stakeholders the goals of the instructional program.

b. Performance objectives can be presented in complete detail or can be summarized in more general terms depending on the needs and interests of different types of stakeholders.

c. Performance objectives provide a solid basis for the precise planning of the test items, instructional materials, and instructional delivery system to be developed for the program.

d. Performance objectives serve as the ultimate criterion for the effectiveness of the program, allowing evaluators to determine whether and how well the program works.

25. (obj. 13) Describe one advantage and one disadvantage of doing an educational research and development (R&D) project for a thesis or dissertation study.

Answer (any 1 from each set OK):

Advantages

a. A good educational R&D project not only contributes to educational research, but it also can lead directly to improvements in educational practice through the application of the program that was developed.

b. An educational R&D project gives the researcher the opportunity to learn more about development, as well as about research.

c. An educational R&D project provides an opportunity to compare the effectiveness of two or more alternative instructional programs in operation.

Disadvantages

a. Taking a program though all the stages of the R&D cycle takes a long time.

b. Educational R&D projects usually require funds and staff beyond the capability of most graduate students.

c. To conduct a successful educational R&D project the researcher must have not only an adequate level of research skills, but also adequate development skills.

APPLICATION PROBLEMS

Problem 1

A friend of yours, who is the director of a new program to aid migrant students and their families in the region, is preparing an annual budget. She asks you, as someone who has conducted educational evaluations, to help her decide how much money, if any, should be spent on program evaluation. She realizes that the less spent on evaluation, the more funds that will be available for direct program operations. What arguments can you present in favor of allocating at least 10 percent of the program budget for program evaluation?

<u>Sample Answer:</u>

   a. As the director she will need to make decisions continuously about the program (e.g., whether to reallocate resources, change timelines, or redesign operating procedures). Evaluation can provide data that will improve these decisions.

   b. The director probably is accountable to others (e.g., clients and an executive board) for program results. Evaluation can give the director more valid data about program results than she would have if she relied exclusively on her own or others' subjective impressions.

   c. Having solid information about the program's effectiveness could be a big help in obtaining additional funds for the program from funding sources, such as foundation or government grants.

Problem 2

A curriculum developer plans to conduct a preliminary field test of a set of self-instructional materials designed to improve the writing skills of college freshmen. List questions that the developer might want to have answered about the materials' effectiveness.

<u>Sample Answer:</u>

   a. To what extent do the materials achieve specific performance objectives involving students' writing skills?

   b. Are the materials easy for instructors and students to understand?

   c. Do the materials require more classroom time than is likely to be available in a typical college writing course?

   d. How do typical college instructors feel about the worth of the materials, and what recommendations do they have for improving them?

   e. How do college students judge the worth of the materials, and what recommendations do they have for improving them?

Problem 3

You have been asked by an elementary school principal to conduct an evaluation of the school's three-year-old study skills program. When you ask the principal what aspects of the program he wants to have evaluated, he replies, "I don't know. What do you usually evaluate?" How might you respond to his question?

Sample Answer:

You might point out that most school instructional programs have various components (e.g., for staff development, parent involvement, instructional materials, peer tutoring, and keeping records on student progress). Each component can be evaluated with respect to one or more aspects: its goals, resources, procedures, and management. The principal needs to make a tentative decision about which components and which aspects of the program need to be evaluated, so that you can plan the scope of the effort and have a place to start.

Problem 4

An instructional program has one stated goal--to train high school students who are nonswimmers to swim freestyle two lengths of an Olympic-size pool in under four minutes. You have been asked to evaluate the program, and you believe a goal-free evaluation is the most appropriate evaluation model. How would you approach the task of evaluation?

Sample Answer:

You would not ask for any further details about the program's goal. You would disregard the goal in designing the evaluation and focus instead on the program's actual effects. These effects might include changes in the pool's regular schedule as a result of the new program; other students' expressions of acceptance, avoidance, or ridicule of nonswimmers entered into the program; the extent to which the students swim after the program is completed; and the students' reported fear of swimming, even though they might have achieved proficiency.

TEACHING ACTIVITIES

Activity 1

Assign a research article that reports the evaluation of an educational program. Ask students to write a brief assignment in which they summarize the researcher's decisions and actions in relation to each step in the evaluation process (as described on pp. 682-691 in the textbook).

Activity 2

Distribute the 30 standards from the *Standards for Evaluations of Educational Programs, Projects, and Materials* among your students. Ask students to report in class how well the article used for Activity 1 above met each of the standards, and what changes, if any, could have improved the evaluation study or its reporting.

Activity 3

Bring to class a description of a real or hypothetical educational program (e.g., a textbook, videotape, or computer game) that a development team wants to develop, and have students examine it. Have students use figure 17.3 in the text (the 10-step R&D cycle) to plan the development of the program. If possible, have them carry out at least one specific activity (e.g., develop an actual instructional goal, identify one characteristic of the learners, write one performance objective, etc.) for each step.